Machine Books: operating at the
intersection of digital and print,
publishing work we believe in.

machinebooks.co.uk

How the Olympics
came to East London

PLAY THE GAME

By Michael Owens
and Ralph Ward

MACHINE
BOOKS

Make no little plans;
they have no magic to stir men's blood ...

Daniel Burnham, on the rebuilding of Chicago
after the 1871 fire.

Play The Game
How the Olympics came to East London
By Michael Owens and Ralph Ward

First published in Great Britain
in 2022 by Machine Books

Publisher:
Machine Books

machinebooks.co.uk
ISBN 978-1-7392145-0-0

Book Design and Typesetting:
Manuel Granja
Set in Greta Text Pro and At Hauss Aero

A CIP catalogue record for this book
is available from the British Library

9	Introduction
11	Methodology
13	Dramatis Personae
16	Acronyms
21	I
59	II
103	III
133	IV
149	V
169	Index

Introduction

Just before 10pm on Sunday 5th August 2012, Usain Bolt, shortly to become the fastest man in the world over 100 m, lined up in his starting blocks in the Olympic Stadium. Across the globe the eyes of millions of people focused on the mysterious part of London known, if at all, as the Lower Lea Valley. Ten seconds later, the roar of 80,000 onlookers in the stadium carried across to the Aquatic Centre, the Copper Box Arena, the Velodrome and the Athlete's Village. Heads turned in the Park's numerous temporary venues and green spaces. Satellite images were beamed around the world from the International Broadcasting Centre.

Only ten years earlier, an advisor to the London Mayor visited the proposed Olympic site as London's bid started to gather steam and commented 'what a shithole'. The Lower Lea was then still one of the most remote, abused and neglected parts of the city, known only to a few Londoners beyond the dwindling number of small businesses still operating there, a handful of remaining residents and a disparate collection of allotment holders, hardy cyclists, indiscriminate fishermen, the odd flaneur and a scattering of evangelistic planners, like your authors.

London had chosen its most unglamorous corner as the site for its 2012 Olympic bid. This little book tells some of the story of how this happened, in the words of some of the people involved: people who created the first visionary narratives of what the Lea could become; people who assembled the plans and blagged the investment that began to suggest that radical change might actually be possible; people who, faced with the heroic Olympic challenge, rolled up their sleeves and got on with it. The stories are recorded here as dialogue, based on interviews.

Ralph Ward and Michael Owens

Methodology

We first conducted interviews with contributors in Spring 2015. We met face-to-face in a variety of London cafes, bars and homes. We returned to transcripts in 2021, converting them from raw spoken word into dialogue, seeking legibility and capturing the narrative of the Olympic project. Thank you to Sarah Bartlett for her invaluable help in that painstaking task. We shared the updated accounts with the participants and made further edits to ensure they accurately represent the views of the contributors in 2022. We would like to take this opportunity to thank those who have helped us build up this collaged picture of how a new part of London was planned.

Ralph Ward and Michael Owens

Dramatis Personae

Gareth Blacker

> During the Olympics Gareth was Director of Development at the LDA, responsible for the huge Olympic Park land assembly, compulsory purchase and relocations programme, as well as the initial legacy masterplan. He is now Director of Strategic Development & Infrastructure at the Homes and Communities Agency.

Mark Bostock

> Mark joined consultants Arup to set up their economic consultancy in 1980. He played a key role in determining the route and alignment for the Channel Tunnel Rail Link through Stratford, and developing the initial plans for Stratford City. Mark led the Mayor's feasibility study into holding the Olympics in the Lea Valley, which provided the foundation for the Olympic bid.

Paul Brickell

> Paul has been an influential presence in the Lower Lea area since the 1990s, and remains so today. In the 1990s he was an early and active member of the Bromley by Bow Centre, before becoming the Chief Executive of the Leaside Regeneration Company, as well as being an elected member of Newham Council. Today he is the Executive Director for Regeneration and Community Partnerships for the London Legacy Development Corporation.

Richard Brown

> Richard worked for the GLA as Private Secretary to the Mayor, Ken Livingstone, and then as Manager of the Mayor's Architecture and Urbanism Unit. As the bid became increasingly serious he followed the action, first to the DCMS and then ODA. He was Director of Strategy for London Legacy Development Corporation from 2009 to 2014 From then until 2021 he was the Deputy Director of the Centre for London, and is now a freelance writer and consultant on urban issues.

Neale Coleman

Neale was appointed by Ken Livingstone as his Olympic advisor right at the very start of the preparation of the bid in 2003. He was on the panels that selected the masterplanners and key Board and Executive personnel. He was a board Member of the ODA, and Deputy Chair of the London Legacy Development Corporation, as well as being a member of just about every management group that had 'Olympic' in their name.

Eleanor Fawcett

In the build up to the Games, Eleanor worked for the GLA's Architecture and Urbanism Unit and later the Design for London team, and was instrumental in a wide range of influential planning and development projects which sought to enhance the identity and quality of the Lea Valley and the so called 'fringe' area beyond the Olympic Park. The White Building in Hackney Wick is one of them. Three Mills Green is another. She is now Head of Design at the Old Oak Common and Park Royal Development Corporation.

James Graven

Before the Olympics, the LDA recruited James as a consultant from PricewaterhouseCoopers to increase their general project management capacity. This turned out to be a masterstroke. He was central to the planning and management of the LDA's Olympic programme. He is now a partner in Deloitte, leading their Real Estate team.

Sandra Hunt

Sandra was Regeneration Adviser to the Chief Executive at Newham Council in the mid 1990s, and then Assistant Chief Executive. When Lea Valley planning was still in its infancy, she led the creation of the vision for Stratford, Lower Lea and the Royal Docks, called 'the Arc of Opportunity', and drove it forward. More than anything else this is what got the Lea Valley ball rolling.

Michael Keith

A Tower Hamlets Councillor for over 20 years and a former Council Leader, Michael played a large and active part in developing the Council's regeneration plans and priorities. His parallel academic life at Goldsmiths and at Queen Mary College, University of London focused on urban issues. Today he holds a personal chair in the Department of Anthropology in the University of Oxford, is the Director of the PEAK Urban Research Programme and co-director of the Oxford programme for the Future of Cities.

Conor McAuley

Conor was an elected Newham councillor for over 34 years from 1984 to 2018, and Executive Member for Regeneration and Strategic Planning for the critical period from 2002 to 2014. From the very early days he played a major part in their initiatives to promote the Borough and attract new development. Between 2012 and 2014 he was a member of the LLDC Planning Committee.

Jason Prior

During the Olympics Jason headed up the EDAW team that created the Olympic Park masterplan. He was instrumental in the successful design and delivery of the Queen Elizabeth Olympic Park, leading the masterplan from bid-stage through to legacy. After EDAW and AECOM merged in 2005, he became AECOM's Chief of Buildings and Places. He is now lead partner of Prior and Partners, Masterplanners and Urban Designers.

Vivienne Ramsey

Vivienne was Newham's Head of Development and Building Control prior to the Olympic bid, and in 2004 simultaneously faced two of the largest planning applications in the country, the Olympic Park and Stratford City. In 2006 she was appointed Director of Planning Decisions for the Olympic Development Authority from 2006 to 2012 and then joined the London Legacy Development Corporation as Executive Director of Planning Policy and Decisions from 2012 to 2013.

Richard Rutter

Between 2002 and 2019 Richard was a senior official at British Waterways, and then the Canals and Rivers Trust, working in a range of policy and implementation roles. He led their work on the Lower Lea Valley and their engagement with the Olympics. His early career was with the Lea Valley Regional Park Authority. He is now a freelance regeneration and leisure consultant.

Kevin Whittle

A professional planner who joined Tower Hamlets in 1986, Kevin left as Director of Regeneration in 2000 to join the Thames Gateway Strategic Executive in the Office of the Deputy Prime Minister. He moved on to become policy director of the London Thames Gateway Development Corporation, which was established in 2003 as part of the Thames Gateway project to promote development in the Lower Lea and broaden the potential impact of the Olympics.

Eleanor Young

Eleanor was Mayor Ken Livingstone's Planning Advisor from 2000 to 2008. She led the team that drafted the Mayor's first London Plan, and provided advice on strategic planning proposals. The London Plan was the first planning document to prioritise the Lea Valley as one of London's major 'Opportunity Areas'. Since 2011, Eleanor has worked as a consultant providing strategic advice on housing, infrastructure and regeneration.

Acronyms

BidCo

BidCo was the name given to the company established in 2003 to prepare London's bid for 2012. It was a private sector-led body that incorporated public sector input from the Department of Culture, Media and Sport and the London Development Agency.

BR

British Rail, a state-owned company that operated most of the overground rail transport in the UK from 1965 until 1997. It was privatised in stages between 1994 and 1997. After privatisation, trains were operated by various private companies, while track, signalling and station management was taken over by Railtrack (later brought under public control as Network Rail).

CTRL

The Channel Tunnel Rail Link is a bespoke high speed rail line linking London St Pancras to the Channel Tunnel. It cost £5.8bn to build, and was opened in November 2007. Now referred to as High Speed 1, services are run by Eurostar.

CPO

A Compulsory Purchase Order gives authorities the power to make land acquisitions that are in the proven public interest. A public inquiry in front of an independent inspector is required where landowners object to the compulsory purchase.

DCMS

Department for Digital, Culture, Media and Sport, the lead Government Department for the London Olympics.

DCLG

The Department for Communities and Local Government, during the build up to the Olympics, was the name given to the Government Department leading on urban regeneration. Before that it was known as the Department of the Environment, and then the Office of the Deputy Prime Minister. It is now the Department for Levelling Up, Housing and Communities. Further changes are probably inevitable.

EDAW

EDAW was an international landscape architecture, urban and environmental design firm that operated until 2009, at which point it was absorbed into parent company AECOM, which had purchased it in 2005. Its name derives from an acronym of its original founders in 1939. In 2003 it won the contract to design the London Olympic Park.

EP

English Partnerships was a non-departmental public body and a national regeneration agency established to support sustainable development and growth in England. English Partnerships London was incorporated into the London Development Agency when it was formed in 2000.

GLA

The Greater London Authority is the democratically-elected strategic authority for London, comprising two parts: the Mayor and Assembly. The Mayor has an executive role, setting an overall vision for London and defining clear strategies on a range of issues, while the Assembly members act as scrutineers. The body was established in 2000, after 14 years of London having no strategic governance following the dissolution of the GLC.

GLC

The Greater London Council was the top-tier local government administrative body for Greater London from 1965 to 1986. The GLC was dissolved in 1986 by the Local Government Act 1985 and its powers were devolved to the London boroughs and other entities.

GoL

The Government Office for London represented central government across the capital between 1994 and 2011. It was one of the UK's Government Offices for the English Regions, the primary government vehicle for coordinating government programmes at the regional level.

IOC

The International Olympic Committee is the governing body of the worldwide Olympic movement and has overall responsibility for organising the modern Olympic Games, including Summer, Winter, and Youth events. It is an independent, international, not-for-profit organisation set up in 1904 which among other things selects host cities and specifies what the Games should comprise.

LCR

London and Continental Railways was established in 1994. In 1996 it bid for and won the contract from the UK government to build and operate the Channel Tunnel Rail Link between London and the Channel Tunnel. As part of the deal they received a large area of former British Rail land at Stratford with which to procure development, and which resulted in the Stratford City concept.

LDA

The London Development Agency was the regional development agency for London from July 2000 until March 2012. It was primarily funded by the Government's Department of Trade and Industry to promote urban regeneration and economic development. The agency had its own Board but was accountable to the Mayor of London for its strategic direction and delivery. As such it was part of the Mayor's 'family' of agencies.

LDDC

The London Docklands Development Corporation was an agency set up by the Government in 1981, and operated ultimately under Government control, to regenerate the depressed Docklands area. This part of East London is an area of 22 sq kms covering parts of the London Boroughs of Newham, Tower Hamlets and Southwark. Because it took over key development powers from local authorities, relations between the body and the councils were initially poor, but these had improved by the time it was de-designated in 2000.

LLDC

The London Legacy Development Corporation was formed in 2012, taking over responsibility for the management and development of the Olympic Park post Games. The body is a Mayoral Development Corporation, accountable to the Mayor of London and working closely with government, the Boroughs, other agencies and local communities.

LOCOG

The London Organising Committee of the Olympic and Paralympic Games was the organisation responsible for organising and managing the 2012 event. It was jointly established by the Department for Culture, Media and Sport, the Mayor of London and the British Olympic Association in 2005 and was structured as a private company limited by guarantee. It was chaired by Lord Coe.

LTGDC

The London Thames Gateway Development Corporation was a Government agency set up in 2005, to advance the Government's Thames Gateway strategy and specifically attract new investment to the key areas in the London Gateway, notably the Lea Valley. It was seen as complementary to the Olympic strategy which focused on Stratford. Unlike its predecessor the London Dockland Development Company, it sought to work in partnership with local authorities, and democratically elected councillors were included on the Board. It was de-designated in 2013.

LVRPA

The Lea Valley Regional Park Authority was set up by an Act of Parliament in 1966 to manage the Lea Valley Regional Park, the series of linked open spaces that follow the Lea Valley for some 26 miles from beyond the edge of London almost to the Thames, first identified as a potential park in Abercrombie's London Plan of 1944. The Olympic Park overlaps the Lea Valley Park at its northern end. The authority has taken over management of the Velodrome in legacy.

OAPF

The Opportunity Area Planning Framework was a planning document covering the Lea Valley Opportunity Area as defined in the Mayor's first London Plan in 2004. It specifies in greater detail the potential for development in the area and how this might be encouraged.

ODA

The Olympic Delivery Authority was a body set up by the Department for Culture, Media and Sport, responsible for ensuring the delivery of the Park, venues and infrastructure for the 2012 event. It was established by the London Olympic Games and Paralympic Games Act 2006.

OPLC

The Olympic Park Legacy Company was founded in May 2009 by the Mayor of London Office, the Department for Culture, Media and Sport and the Department for Communities and Local Government as guardians of the legacy of the Olympic Park. The company was half-owned by the Government and half by the Mayor's office. It was reformed in April 2012 as the London Legacy Development Corporation under the control of the Mayor of London.

OPRSG

The Olympic Park Regeneration Steering Group was set up in 2009 to discuss and agree legacy plans for the Olympic Park. It brought together politicians from local, regional and national government for the first time.

SRB

The Single Regeneration Budget was a regeneration programme set up by the Government in 1996 to replace the wide and confusing range of programmes then in existence, thus simplifying the structure of regeneration funding.

UCL

The University College London was founded in 1826, as London University. The main campus is found in the Bloomsbury area of central London, but it has a number of institutes elsewhere in London and is currently building a satellite campus at the Queen Elizabeth II Park.

I

Michael Keith:
> You must have heard the story of Alfred? Alfred banished the Vikings to the east of the River Lea. So historically the boundary between London and the Vikings ran down the River Lea. To the west of the River Lea were the British and to the east were the Barbarians and the Vikings! Plus ça change!

Ralph Ward:
> The Lower Lea Valley may have been little known in 2012, but it had played a significant historic role in the economic growth of the city. The focus for London's industrial revolution, it had been the site of major manufacturing enterprises, including the Stratford Rail Works and Thames Ironworks Shipbuilders. It spawned astonishing technological world firsts, including petrol and plastic. But by the early twentieth century the area was already declining as a manufacturing location. After the war, as the Docks began to close, it suffered badly from the wider manufacturing flight from London. Those businesses that did remain were progressively surrounded by low-grade dumping, recycling, and marginal, sometimes colourful enterprises. (I recall a police detective telling me during an Olympic planning meeting how the amount of counterfeit perfume being sold

out of suitcases in Oxford St had plummeted since the 'blue fence' had gone up round the Olympic construction site.)

By the late 1980s the area had evolved into an unresolved landscape of old industrial buildings and increasingly derelict wastelands, amid the odd remaining factory and pockets of distressed housing. By the mid 1990s, when our action begins, the Lea Valley had perhaps reached its lowest point. It didn't really seem to be part of anywhere, certainly not part of London's World City, and there seemed to be no obvious way forward.

The emerging success of London Docklands, however, began to suggest there may be a market-driven future for East London after all, albeit, at this stage, a rather alien one. Local planners and politicians began to sit up and take notice.

Michael Owens:

A significant part of the Lower Lea, the section on its west bank, lies in Tower Hamlets. In the 1990s, Kevin Whittle worked in several senior positions in Tower Hamlets, becoming their lead officer for regeneration. Michael Keith was a Tower Hamlets Councillor at the time and also for a period the Leader of the Council.

Kevin Whittle:

I joined Tower Hamlets Council in the mid 1980s after working for the Greater London Council (GLC). I was leaving an authority that was quite progressive and joining an authority that wanted to keep its traditional industry. In my first couple of weeks, I was proudly taken by my colleagues in Economic Development to a metal-bashing shed where women were stamping out casters to put on the bottom of beds. They had all the doors open because it was so horribly hot in there. One man ran the place, and the workers were low-paid women. I was told this was what economic development was all about; he was churning out millions of those things.

I was taken aback by Tower Hamlets' attitude towards local economic opportunities and particularly industry — that all jobs were good jobs. And that's what the wider Lea Valley meant to the Council for quite a long time. It was driven by the idea that industry meant working class jobs and that was where real Tower Hamlets people worked, so office work was basically irrelevant.

Michael Keith:

I was a lecturer at Queen Mary University, although my family came from here quite a long time back. My mum's dad worked for the Thames River Police, based in Wapping, so she was born around here. They were all sent off in the war, but I came back here at a time when we still had some family locally. I got involved in local politics because a few of my mates were part of a network of mostly young Bangladeshi boys who were campaigning against various forms of racism, and then the BNP got into power on the Isle of Dogs. These things seemed quite important.

The Liberals, who ran the Council for a period between the mid 1980s and mid 1990s, had established a model of decentralisation, which was meant to bring local government closer to the people. The paradox was that bringing local government closer to the people bred an intense parochialism, which effectively meant that the west of the Borough became intensified around Bangladeshi politics. And east of the Borough, particularly the neighbourhoods of Bromley by Bow, Bow and the Isle of Dogs, became very white in terms of their political identity. What struck me from quite early on was that this was an area of incredibly rapid change and fantastic potential, as well as something that was much more global in scope.

Tower Hamlets was sometimes caricatured as 'the London Borough of Housing', in that housing dominated every agenda. For me, it was important to take a broader perspective, and that shaped my approach to urban regeneration. In terms of Tower Hamlets, what was interesting was that there was a chance to think about an old London economy that had collapsed and a new London global economy that was emerging.

The urban regeneration agenda could be understood as being structured by three things: firstly, there was the dynamics of the city fringe, which, at its crudest, could represent the city rolling eastwards and displacing everybody; secondly, the new world of the financial district of Canary Wharf; and thirdly, this great big slab of old manufacturing in London, which was the River Lea.

It seemed to me that there was a failure of both the old left and the old right models in addressing this process of economic restructuring. Very crudely, it meant trying to sustain the city fringe as somewhere to live and work simultaneously, without being rolled over by the forces of gentrification around the city, moving east.

Michael Owens:

In 1981, the London Docklands Development Corporation (LDDC) took control of land in the Isle of Dogs from Tower Hamlets Council and started the process that would ultimately see Canary Wharf generate over 180,000 office jobs by 2022. Back in the 1980s, however, the first glass towers appeared to have landed from another country, irrelevant to the needs of the traditional working class neighbourhoods of East London. Male unemployment in Newham stood at 30% in 1984, and the new white collar jobs seemed immaterial to those who had lost work as the dock and manufacturing industries collapsed.

Michael Keith:

At Canary Wharf, it was about trying to say that this wasn't an island ghetto that people moved into from the rest of London and the south east of England, but that it was part of the landscape here in Tower Hamlets, and so we needed metaphorically and literally to break down the walls.

And in terms of what happened on the River Lea, we were trying to think what a new economy might be, how it could replace what had gone before and how it could generate real economic growth along with some form of redistributive benefit for what was already there.

Kevin Whittle:

The LDDC was established by the Government in 1981 to regenerate the dockland areas of East London. The LDDC boundary was drawn in the early 1980s and the Lower Lea Valley was not within it. Some thought was subsequently given in the late 1980s to extending the LDDC remit to include the Lower Lea Valley. But a consultant report basically said of the Lower Lea: 'don't go there; it's too difficult.' The thinking at that time was that you might get the private sector interested in Docklands because you're putting in all this government land, with massive subsidies, and you're building public transport — so you're providing a huge amount of public sector investment to drag them in. But you don't own the Lower Lea Valley, so you've got to acquire it. The Government could have acquired the land there using CPO (Compulsory Purchase Order) powers, but you can't just take it from private owners. And there was no obvious future in the Lower Lea Valley and Stratford in terms of marketability, so there was no point. The LDDC didn't go there — they left it. And I think what's interesting is that there are lots of examples right up to the present time where there's been a general feeling among the great and the good — the dinner-party lot, you know, who decide what policies are going to happen — that the Lower Lea Valley and Stratford were just awful places, and it was never going to happen.

As planning authority and major land owner, the LDDC stuck rigidly to the planning application consultation period, 21 days I think in those days. But the Boroughs were unlikely to get their act together to respond to anything in 21 days. So Tower Hamlets just objected to everything, as a matter of course. Politically, relations weren't good, although behind the scenes a lot of productive work went on.

Ralph Ward:

The GLC had been abolished and London was languishing without metropolitan leadership. Strategic planning was in the hands of the Government Office for London (GoL), but what sounds like a recipe for abject inertia turned out to be the opposite. Driven by John Sienkiewicz, the strategic planning lead in GoL, London's most creative planner of his time and hugely influential with both politicians and major developers, a new cadre of local planners and politicians were encouraged to think for themselves, and develop local strategies that might re-energise local communities and combine private sector-led physical renewal with social regeneration. In 1994 the Lea Valley became designated as an Objective 2 area, eligible for generous EU grants to attract new investment and jobs, because of the decline in employment. GoL created a new partnership of East London local authorities, known as the Lea Valley Partnership, to jointly manage this grant programme. But also on the horizon was a national policy initiative called the Thames Gateway which was launched by the Secretary of State for the Environment in 1995. This confusingly overlapped the designated Lea Valley area, and Thameside boroughs found it rather more politically interesting.

Kevin Whittle:
>The Lower Lea was not a priority in terms of national or local politics in the early 1990s. Interestingly, the whole concept of London being 'needy' enough to qualify for Objective 2 status was initially unacceptable to central government. Lower Lea Valley Partnership had been formed by local authorities with some encouragement by GoL but it was falling apart; the idea of supporting inward investment did not win automatic local political support. Community politics was important, in the context of the Boroughs winning big money at the time in response to levels of poverty and deprivation.
>
>Irate politicians, particularly in Tower Hamlets, were saying, 'hang on a minute, you've won this because of Bengali poverty, so give it to the Bengalis. What are you doing? The bloody marketing costs millions! We want more housing but we can't spend it on housing! We want more windows and we can't spend it on windows!'
>
>There was a lot of animosity, and it was hard to handle. You've got Boroughs who each have their own core focus. The Lea Valley belonged to nobody. Newham was promoting two main development zones: the Royal Docks in the south of the borough and Stratford. Hackney was promoting Dalston and Hoxton. And Tower Hamlets was at full blast trying to do something around Spitalfields. No one was interested in the Lea Valley.

Ralph Ward:
>Conor McAuley was former lead member for regeneration at the London Borough of Newham. He also recalls the atmosphere of the time within the so-called Partnership and the absence of any collective cross-borough strategic thinking.

Conor McAuley:
>In the mid 1990s, the government-sponsored Lea Valley Partnership included all the councils with land in the Lea

Valley, along with several stakeholders. We never got on with the guys in the north of the partnership though. There were always tensions, even at all the Channel Tunnel Rail Link (CTRL) events in Stratford. These guys would turn up and they'd all go, 'ugh, just banging on about Stratford again.' There was always a sense of envy about it. We always seemed rather good at what we did, and we only ever talked about Stratford, for which we make no apology.

Michael Owens:
> Conservative Minister Michael Heseltine led the creation of the London Docklands Development Corporation in the 1980s. Later in 1991, he launched a new urban regeneration model called City Challenge. Local authorities, working in partnership with local community organisations and businesses, would compete to secure £37.5m to spend on the regeneration of their area over five years. Locally, Newham Council competed for the funds in 1991 and again in 1992. The bid under the second round was successful. The resulting Stratford Development Partnership, led by the charismatic Chief Executive Steve Jacobs, would invest in a number of projects in Stratford and the east side of the Lea Valley. In Tower Hamlets, a successful City Challenge bid was also made for Bethnal Green.
>
> The successor to City Challenge was the Single Regeneration Budget (SRB), which began in 1994. Tower Hamlets bid successfully into the first round of Single Regeneration Budget to fund the 'Cityside' urban regeneration programme in the west of the Borough. Later rounds of the SRB would see the creation of the Leaside Regeneration Company, providing funds for urban regeneration projects on the west side of the Lower Lea Valley. In 1998, I took up the position of Chief Executive of the newly formed company, working to the Board.

Michael Keith:

> The future of the Lea was always something that was: (a) up for grabs, and (b) put on the table by the broader government and sub-regional context. There was a Lea Valley Partnership, which seemed to be a complete mess. Before the Olympics, the strategic regional planning logic centred on either the Lea Valley as an axis of economic growth or the Thames Gateway. And at the time that was partly a political distinction.
>
> It was quite an interesting moment when we effectively brought together the Lea Valley Partnership and Thames Gateway Partnership, in the end de facto killing the old vehicle of Lea Valley Partnership. This led to the creation of the Thames Gateway beast, with a bureaucracy as big as a secondary school attached to it.
>
> But for us, just getting Tower Hamlets to think beyond the villages of the bloody Hamlets was hard enough. We had Bethnal Green City Challenge, which is in the west of the Borough. Part of the parochialism was that every small part of the bloody Borough wanted its own piece of whatever initiative was going on elsewhere in the Borough.
>
> The Government wanted to draw Tower Hamlets into its investment strategy for the Lower Lea. The day that England played the Netherlands in Euro 96 was the day that Kevin Whittle, then my Director of Regeneration, got John Sienkiewicz of the GoL to meet him and me in Gabriel's Wharf, at which point a lot of bottles of wine were drunk. I was more keen on watching the football: England beat Netherlands, and Shearer scored a hat-trick. I quite liked Sienkiewicz — he was that kind of 'fuck you, bloody politicians' type, which was not always easy. But I gave up watching the football match to sit and talk with him and Whittle about creating an arms-length vehicle for the Lea Valley. It was a Faustian bargain.

Our Chief Executive at the time, Sylvie Pearce, had gone to Sienkiewicz and said, 'look, we need to get some regeneration money.' They gave us a tiny bit of money to produce a planning framework for the Lower Lea, produced by the masterplanners Llewelyn Davies. One view was that the market was going to do all this anyway, so why would we need a special planning framework? And Kevin Whittle said, 'the market's not going to do it.' Frankly, we needed the planning framework as a symbolic thing, you know. They could have written a bastardised Latin version of the Magna Carta, and if it was labelled 'Lea Valley' it would at least have been a flag that you could then stick on the map to say, 'this is something that you can actually do here.'

Bluntly, we needed a succession strategy for the Bethnal Green City Challenge for the west of the Borough, something to happen in the Lea Valley for the east of the Borough, and to cut a deal with the LDDC and Canary Wharf as to what was going to happen in the LDDC area. All at the same time! To be honest, whether it was looking north and south for the Lea Valley or east and west for the Thames Gateway, was neither here nor there at that point. It was far worse than that. It was much more parochial.

Ralph Ward:

As London was beginning to wise up to the potential which its East End offered the city, so did important parts of Central Government. Michael Heseltine was rather proud of what his Docklands had achieved, and prompted by his adviser Peter Hall and by Mark Bostock, then planning lead at engineers Arup, he focused a new national policy of growth and change further east again, along the moribund Thames Estuary, now rebranded as the Thames Gateway. At the time, a rail link to the Channel Tunnel was being planned by the Department of Transport to run through south London. Mark Bostock suggested that a radically new route for CTRL along the estuary could form the spine of the Gateway strategy and he set out with his team at Arup to draw up a proposal. This included a new international station at Stratford. Were this to be linked to Canary Wharf by the projected Jubilee Line, who knows what might happen then?

Newham Council were quick to put their support behind it, and their confidence in what Stratford could become grew rapidly. But there was still a great deal of prejudice and indifference to overcome.

Mark Bostock:

A lot has been written about the role that Arup took in challenging the Government's proposals for linking the Channel Tunnel portal with London. This is not the place to discuss this extraordinary story as it has been well covered in Nicholas Faith's book, appropriately titled *The Right Line: The Politics, The Planning And The Againgst-The-Odds Gamble Behind Britain's First High-Speed Line* (Segrave Faulks, 2007). He wrote:

'The fast rail line was a once-in-a-century opportunity, and it was only fully grasped by a lucky combination of two far-sighted politicians, from different parties and at different times, and a group of imaginative engineers. In this improbable trio were two deputy prime ministers, Michael Heseltine and John Prescott; the third member, Arup, is the engineering consultancy founded in 1946 by the engineer-extraordinaire Ove Arup. Without the involvement of these three at crucial moments, a completed rail line, and in the best place, would never have emerged from a primaeval swamp of official muddle and ideological posturing.'

I include this because in recent years Michael Heseltine quotes him and me as being the two buccaneers in this story. By chance, we happened to be around at the same time after I had set up the economics and planning business in Arup and whilst I was leading the three-man team charged with identifying the Arup alignment to challenge the BR route.

Michael Owens:

British Rail (BR) had for decades been working on proposals for the Channel Tunnel Rail link. In 1989, after years of struggling to identify a preferred and viable route or alignment as it is known in the business, BR published a preferred alignment, based on a business case centred on revenues from passenger services. Meanwhile Mark Bostock and Arup were working with partners on another proposal and hoping to secure BR's backing for it. Arup explored alternative routes with a business case that generated value from property development and freight services.

One consequence of the alignment published by BR was that a long tunnel from Swanley would emerge at the surface at Warwick Gardens in Peckham, where it would join existing lines into Waterloo. The location would be further complicated and a locally valued green space blighted by a proposed link to Kings Cross at the same point. A vociferous campaign against the alignment would be taken up by residents in the steadily gentrifying Peckham Rye neighbourhoods. Arup would go out on a limb and eventually win the case for an alignment through Stratford and east London into Kings Cross.

Mark Bostock:

Lord Heseltine and I connected and created the outcome, which in Lord Heseltine's view brought the whole development of the Lower Lea and the Thames Gateway into perspective. Firstly, in terms of the development of London Docklands, and getting its structure, financing and delivery right. Secondly — with Arup being the architect, not in the physical sense, but in terms of leadership — challenging the Government on its alignment and ending up with the preferred alignment connecting London with the Channel Tunnel from the east via Stratford.

It's very interesting for me to re-read Malcolm Rifkind's statement in the House of Commons, on the 9th October 2001, as to why the Government chose our alignment as opposed to the one put forward by British Rail. On the one hand, you've got an engineering design for a straight-line fast railway linking the Channel Tunnel portal with Waterloo, with an extension to King's Cross destroying a large area around Peckham. And on the other, ours which had value in terms of both transport and regeneration.

Construction costs weren't significantly different to the British Rail option that was on the table, although the engineering risk was significantly different as the BR scheme involved tunnelling under south-west London which was not through London clay. But our alignment had much wider benefits, not just transport. And it was the regenerative value of coming into London from the east via Stratford that was the winner — the catalytic effect that it would have on both Stratford and Ebbsfleet, these being the two intermediate stations that were finally decided upon. This was reflected in the Secretary of State's statement and I have taken the liberty of quoting from his statement:

'... we have decided that a route on the lines put forward by Ove Arup which approaches central London from the east, via Stratford ... would satisfy our transport objectives by providing additional capacity when it is needed. Moreover, it would minimise the impact of the line on the environment and on residential property ... we recognised the substantial potential that it offered for development along the east Thames corridor. The new line could serve as an important catalyst for plans for the regeneration of that corridor ...'

Despite the excitement I experienced with this announcement, I must tell you how frustrating it was because, having won the battle and the case, we were truncated in terms of our ambition. Originally we had two double twin tracks coming in from the area around the Medway. This allowed us to plan one set of tracks coming into Barking through London Docklands, going up to Stratford and joining up with the Cambridge line. And we had the other set going through London, underneath King's Cross with the trains pointing north in order to connect either with the West Coast Main Line or the Midlands Main Line. And we also had Crossrail playing into that — a truly connected railway!

Our objective at Stratford was to create a highly significant modal and transport interchange — the hub for East London. Our original proposition was to have the alignment with the high speed railway in parallel with the regional railway to get the best synergies. That was our dream but that is what we were unable to deliver and I'm very sorry about that.

Our original proposition also had slightly different intermediate stations. Stratford was always a given, despite opposition from the Department of Trade and British Rail. Right up to the time when the line was bid for by the three or four contenders, Stratford was an option but we insisted on it. We also insisted on a connection with the West Coast Main Line immediately north of the lines at Kings Cross/St Pancras. We wanted to provide for trains to Europe coming down from Birmingham via Stratford, as we had from Kings Cross/St Pancras via Ebbsfleet. That was our vision. And it was very sad that we couldn't deliver that, because of the political environment in which we were operating. This was a great disappointment as it meant that Stratford was not going to develop on the scale we had hoped; nor was it going to easily connect with the Eurostar train services because the closeness of Stratford with St Pancras/Kings Cross meant that it made no commercial sense to have Stratford included in a stopping service for a high speed train with eighteen carriages.

As we were putting the lines through Stratford, Stuart Lipton and others retained Arup to produce a master plan for Stratford City, a combination that got Westfield to consider putting a retail complex between the two stations, which I thought was amazing. As we were lobbying we discovered that the Department of Environment, with Michael Heseltine as the Secretary of State, had brought in an extremely bright adviser in the form of Professor Peter Hall. He was hugely important because he had already grasped the significance of this area and could see how these lines coming in would be transformational.

Arup, having risked money on my team and associated public affairs costs, realised that we would have to compete to deliver the railway on our alignment. Nicholas Wakefield, S G Warburg & Co and I set up London and Continental Railways as a transport company to bid for the concession to build, own and operate the new high speed railway line and to own European Passenger Services, later to be known as Eurostar. Nick and I quickly brought together an outstanding group of shareholders. This included Virgin (because of their interest in operating Eurostar trains as if they were 'jumbo jets'), National Express (because of their transport management expertise), S G Warburg & Co, the merchant bank (later acquired by UBS), Bechtel for Project Management, Halcrow and Arup for their design skills and latterly London Electricity, and Systra, the consultancy arm of SNCF (French Railways).

We intended to take our proposition to the private sector, because naively we thought sufficient income would come in from Eurostar. We also thought that would create sufficient cash for us to raise an IPO (Initial Public Offering) on the London Stock Market. Eurostar had not yet completed its first year of operations and we had three or four problems there. First, low-cost airlines started coming in and we hadn't planned on that. Second, which is the problem with Stratford today, is that the trains were huge single items: big chunks of metal, 400 metres long. As an investment they were very inflexible, with high fixed costs. You couldn't send them off and cut them in half or quarters or tenths to respond to low levels of demand. So the inflexibility of the asset and its high fixed cost was a problem. The reason why these big trains can't stop at Stratford now is that for them to slow down and then to accelerate in that short distance to travel to St Pancras is just not commercially viable. So today Stratford International has only got four platform faces. It's very small. It's a great shame. As already explained we envisaged it as much bigger. It's a big missed opportunity. Despite my disappointment over the failure for the Department of Transport to grasp the full impact of our original proposition, I do have to reflect a little on the impact of the Arup alignment. I remember at a reception in Westfield when the shopping complex was under construction, gazing out over Stratford towards what is now called the Queen Elizabeth Olympic Park, someone tapped me on the shoulder and said: 'you know you are responsible for all this and in economic terms you are responsible for contributing at least £25 billion to the national economy'.

Conor McAuley:
In the 1990s, Stratford started to emerge as a potentially important location. I think two key issues predate the late-1990s visions for the Lower Lea but influence them completely. One was the CTRL, when British Rail, as it then was, announced in about 1998 that they were going to build a rail link to the Channel Tunnel with one or two terminals in London. They were discussing a list of locations they might examine. White City was one, King's Cross, Waterloo and

Stratford. They went down a two-year evaluation process to decide where these terminals should be.

This came out of the blue at Newham. 'Oh, Stratford, that's interesting.' But before we even got our heads around it, they said, 'we're going to do Waterloo, and we'll do the next one at King's Cross.' So they abandoned the process. And we thought, 'hang on a minute! Stratford was quite a good idea.'

At that point there was still a lot of argument over where the route of the Channel Tunnel would go, whether it would come through South London, splitting at a place called Warwick Garden, underneath Lewisham I think, with lines then going up to King's Cross and Waterloo. Or down the estuary route that came in from the east.

The east route suited Newham; it suited Stratford. We got behind the eastern route and started lobbying for Stratford, initially, to be the terminal. And when it became clear that King's Cross had to happen, we began to consider how Stratford might be brought forward as a station along the route, and we got a taste for working through what the options might be. We all believed, and we still do, that regeneration follows transport infrastructure. We started to think about what you could do in Stratford if you had a Channel Tunnel station.

It's funny thinking back to all those parallel things that took place. When the Government chose the estuary route for the CTRL, they ditched the idea of a station at Stratford. At no point did they put it into legislation; it was just an aspiration. And it didn't happen until Prescott came along and made it a requirement to put a station at Stratford.

To encourage them to build the station at Stratford, we put together a group of developers who were willing to build the station for free. We did that and a number of other things to try and get the station at Stratford. In fairness to John Prescott, it was his decision that the station would get built, but he never gets the credit for it.

Unrelated to the Channel Tunnel, around the same time, the City of London wanted to move Spitalfields fruit and vegetable market out to where they are now, in Leyton, a short distance north of Stratford up the Lea Valley. There was already a fruit and vegetable market in Stratford, off Stratford High Street, on land now occupied by the Jubilee Line depot. Of course, prior to 1990 there was no Jubilee Line. Together with Fred Jones, the leader of the Council at the time, and with John Burrows, our Assistant Chief Executive, who was the guy who did all the regeneration planning at this time, we thought we would bid to locate Spitalfields market in Stratford.

That was the first time we sought to bid to change people's minds on something. We identified a site, partly on land that we owned, now the Jubilee Line depot, and put that in as a bid. We knew that if Spitalfields moved, Stratford market would close. There was no logic to having two fruit and vegetable markets in East London. Although it didn't work out and we didn't win — they chose to move it to Leyton — the experience showed us that we could do those things.

The developer had been keen to work with us, and with the experience gained, we formed the idea that we could do something at Stratford with the CTRL. We launched a lengthy campaign about the rail link. I remember being on the board of the LDDC in 1990, and at various times they thought we were insane. But we got there.

When Canary Wharf Limited started lobbying for the Jubilee line extension, the issue was where was that going to go? There was the option to go out to Stratford, or to go out to Woolwich. And there was a debate. We obviously got behind the Stratford option, as did Canary Wharf Limited, because they could see that that was where the young population was, and they wanted to connect with the growth east of Stratford.

We were part of a successful argument to bring the Jubilee Line to Stratford, which reinforced the CTRL argument. These things were coming together. And then in 1995 — this is a good time to start — David Curry became Housing Minister, and this has particularly stuck in my memory. He made that speech about delivering 203,000 new houses that housing ministers do in every era, but one of the places he specifically mentioned in his speech was the Lower Lea Valley. And we all said, 'Hang on a minute. We're not putting all this effort into the CTRL and all these other things just so David Curry can cover all the land in houses.' Housing is important, obviously, but we were looking for employment regeneration for East London as well. So that's why we redoubled our efforts to think what we could do at Stratford, if we had CTRL, rather than just cover it in housing.

And just to canter through all this quickly, around the same time there was a competition for a site to hold a millennium celebration. People forget that three were on the final shortlist: Birmingham, the Greenwich Peninsula and Stratford. A bid for Stratford was written in an afternoon in Steve Jacob's office (CEO of Stratford City Challenge) at The Old Dispensary in Stratford; there were three of us there. There were 61 bids from across the country and to get to the final three genuinely astonished us. We only found out when the press started banging on the door at Steve Jacob's office wanting to do an interview.

It was all about creating momentum for what could be done at Stratford, not just plopping down housing. The vision we would go on to develop for the Arc of Opportunity was also part of that; it was knitting together what we wanted to do at Stratford and the Lower Lea Valley, right round through to the Royal Docks, because although the LDDC were there, there had been two recessions and they had missed the opportunities to get things moving. We created the

Arc of Opportunity competition, initially an architectural competition, to spark interest in that whole area, including the Royal Docks and Stratford.

Michael Owens:

In the early 1990s Vivienne Ramsey was Head of Development and Building Control at Newham Council. She was in charge of the team processing planning applications and worked very closely with other areas of planning and regeneration to help develop a corporate vision for Stratford. We met Vivienne with her colleague from the period, Michael Heraty. He was part of the regeneration team, working on planning and development projects and also working with the newly formed Stratford City Challenge partnership.

Vivienne Ramsey:

Stratford in the 1980s and 1990s was as unfashionable as you could get, but for Newham it was a target for renewal.

Newham Council would always go for any funding available — European funding, whatever. We were sensible enough to have the flexibility to allow partners to come on board. We were serious. If you've got the money, we'd like to help shape your ideas about how we could go about doing this. We always had some aim in view, or some objectives that we were trying to get towards, but recognising that to take advantage of opportunities that came along we'd have to deviate in some way.

The City Challenge offered an opportunity for some significant projects that could be used to advertise Stratford. The new bus station was one of those: knock down the old multi-storey car park and bus station, which was horrible. It stank; it was disgusting. The new design, bright and cheerful, became the new poster asset that you could use to advertise Stratford. It was an in-house design for Stratford bus station by Transport for London (TfL), a pretty good, striking design. That led to people concentrating their minds on Stratford rail station, which to put it mildly was a hole in the ground. There was no station entrance whatsoever to the town centre. It was like a drain. You came through to the back of it through a subway, under a road, and the ticket office was a hole in the wall at the end. Or you went into a taxi turnaround car park down some steps into the end of the subway. It was just horrible.

When the plans for the Jubilee Line extension coming through to Stratford were put on the table, they were doing great things at Canada Water, and there were attractive designs for the stations along the route. Even Canning Town was to have an interchange. They got to West Ham and the brief to the architects was that it had to be vandal-proof because around here they're a bunch of oiks. Great.

They came to show us the designs for Stratford. The design was basically just a platform, a ticket barrier, and a signing-on block for drivers next to the platform. They didn't address any of the core station problems. It was just an add-on, hopelessly inadequate, and it was not going to work. They needed a fundamental redesign. But who the hell was going to fund it? We begged, stole and borrowed from just about every pot that was going. We bid to the European Regional Development Fund, and we bid for new City Challenge money. We basically drew money from everywhere to get a proper station design with proper integration of interchange, facilities and services. And again, one that was a landmark architectural statement for the town centre.

To win your bid you needed a vision, didn't you? What was the big idea for Stratford at the time? Was there a big idea? It was about trying to improve what was already a well-connected place, but people didn't recognise it as such. We had the Docklands Light Railway. The Jubilee Line was on its way. It was about trying to build on that. We said we needed to rebuild the town centre. We were already trying to do just that when I joined Newham Council in 1979.

Our propositions were focused on the community as well as on physical projects. There was community involvement, such as collaborations with local artists who worked with communities, young people and elderly people, to help run projects and design pieces of art like the railway sculpture. There was major investment in housing stock as well. Everyone thinks councils in the East End did bugger all. But it's not true.

The key thing that needed doing was to get people to recognise it as a place. In my early days in Newham, I'd be saying to people, 'there's this brilliant site.' And they would say, 'where is Newham? Isn't it in Essex? It's a long way away.' And I would say, 'you get on a train to Liverpool Street and it's ten minutes to Stratford. Or get the Central Line to Stratford. It hardly takes any time at all.' All they knew was West Ham United, and if you were lucky, and they were a bit more middle class, they would know the Theatre Royal, Stratford East. Those were the only two things they knew.

At what point did Stratford become a serious contender? In a sense we take that for granted now. During the time of the City Challenge, we were kicking off the CTRL campaign as well. When the line between London and Paris was first proposed, it was routed south of the river. Newham joined with Greenwich, other East London boroughs, and cities in the Midlands, to say, 'move it north of the river, do a station at Stratford, and connect all these places that need regeneration. And by the way, chaps, there's this great big area of land around where an international station is going to go, and we really need to put it on the map because people don't know it's there.' Because what we really needed, after all the docks closed, and all the heavy industry had gone, was more jobs.

Once things started to happen, there was a lot more belief and interest in the place. It was a complete bloody wasteland before the City Challenge. But if you look at Stratford now, it's fundamentally changed. Whether the local people have benefited is another matter.

Conor McAuley:

What happened was that the Jubilee Line was coming into Stratford but they had no plans to revamp Stratford station. They were just going to plug it in around the existing platforms, and I said, 'you can't do that.' We started working with partners to put together a cocktail of funding. A lot of transport-support-grant money, European money, the whole thing, which led to the WilkinsonEyre-designed station concourse we have now. If Newham hadn't taken the risk, we would have been lost. Nobody else was prepared to take that risk.

I turned down the planning application for the redesign of West Ham station on the Jubilee Line. We had very little planning power because it was all in the Government's Act of 1993, which gave London Underground the powers to acquire land and construct the Jubilee Line. But I thought the design for West Ham was rubbish. I mean, there are all those wonderful cathedrals at Canary Wharf and North Greenwich, but once you cross into Newham, you've got all these rubbish stations. And so we turned down their plan for West Ham in order to get Stratford right. Because they were never going to spend money on good design east of the Lea.

Edwin Shirley, a businessman in the trucking industry with a close involvement in the music business, was on the board of the City Challenge Company — that's how I got to work with him — as was Richard Reynolds from Barratts, and they both did very well throughout. There were a few people like that who got it. Some of the guys at Union Rail who were doing Channel Tunnel Rail Link work got it as well, but their head offices were saying, 'we're not doing anything here that will interfere with our major project.'

Westfield turned up, as part of what was a consortium for the Stratford City development. I also remember the Reuben brothers, who were with Stewart Lipton. And Lend Lease was part of it as well. There were four entities there. But it was a very unstable partnership, and I remember Robin Wales, Newham's Mayor, and myself refereeing between the partners in Robin's office. In the end it was Westfield who came out on top and won the bid. Stratford City was granted planning consent before the Olympic bid even went in, of course. People forget that.

I remember when Westfield did their presentation to us. They genuinely hadn't worked out which area of London they were targeting; the spending power they were looking for.

It wasn't the first time that work like that needed to be done. Back in the LDDC days, at Beckton Gas Works, a retail operator thought there'd be a river crossing and that he could build a decent shopping centre there, to rival Lakeside and Bluewater. We were all relying on there being a bridge. And he showed us his research identifying where the money was in London, because the LDDC were a bit sceptical, and you know, the developers had done their work. Westfield's plan for Stratford works was very similar, only Westfield relied more on public transport, which was good, so I was familiar with their thinking.

Westfield were very convincing. We went along with their thinking and they were spectacularly right. People were saying it would never work in East London. I'd meet them again and again, all middle-class Labour Party people who were still claiming that people would never go to Westfield. And I'd say, 'well you're just an idiot. It may not be to your taste, but it bloody well works.'

There was always nervousness about how the old Stratford town centre and the new Westfield centre would work together. For my money, far from Westfield being a magnet for attracting middle-class people from all over Greater London, Essex and Kent, it's a working-class shopping centre, an affluent working-class shopping centre, in a really good way. I occasionally took the Overground to Gospel Oak, to go to Hampstead Heath. You could go round to Hampstead Heath that way. We stood at the platform and watched people getting off the train, on their way from Westfield Stratford, and I was thinking, 'why aren't you going to the one in Hammersmith?' I've been to the one at Hammersmith and it feels quite different.

Ralph Ward:

As Newham's ambitions for Stratford and the Lea Valley started to be taken seriously and, in the case of CTRL, to be realised, both they and Tower Hamlets, and new community-based organisations in Tower Hamlets in particular, became increasingly imaginative and confident about the kind of future they might be able to build for the area. Strategies for the Valley, that might not long ago have sounded like crazy fantasies, began to take on the character of serious, plausible propositions. The Lea Valley as a 'Water City' built round a new London focus for Higher Education? Great idea! An 'Arc of Opportunity' for high quality waterside development fronting the River Lea. Why not?

Conor McAuley:

The Arc of Opportunity was a vision and a strategy that knitted together what we wanted to do at Stratford and the Lower Lea Valley, right round through to the Royal Docks, because although the LDDC was there, there had been two recessions and they had missed the opportunities to get things moving. We created the Arc of Opportunity competition, initially an architectural competition, to spark interest in that whole area, including the Royal Docks and Stratford.

Why was the Arc going to the east (Newham) side of the Lea and not the west (Tower Hamlets)? Because on the east side of the Lea, you had all those noxious industries that couldn't exist in what was originally the London County Council area. That's where your gas producer was, your perfume manufacturer, your oil refiner. All those noxious industries, that the Council wouldn't have in its boundary, were east of the river.

So we had all those increasingly redundant sites on our side of the Lea, more than Tower Hamlets, and we wanted to unlock those sites. And because transport corridors through the Lower Lea were east-west, and they were separate from roads like the A13, the hardest thing to do was to travel north-south on the river. We wanted to find some way of linking them, so people could look at Stratford and the Lower Lea and say, 'actually, this is a place.' Otherwise, you'd just drive through it and you wouldn't understand the area. So that's why we were planning to do things that may have seemed illogical.

That's why Three Mills Studios got built. Three Mills was a section of land owned by the Lea Valley Regional Park Authority (LVRPA), which they had abandoned. And there were two full-sized football pitches and changing rooms, among other things, including the nice old buildings that are over there.

I got dragged in around 1985, when the Head of Planning at the time, Diana Kershaw, said to me one day, 'you must come down and look at Three Mills.' And I said, 'where's that?' I had no idea. She took me along, and I was amazed at all the land that was there. It was fantastic! And when we realised that the Lea Valley Park planners didn't care about it, I joined the board of the LVRPA for four years, and we started bringing in ideas. Then the City Challenge programme came in, and we drew the City Challenge bid boundaries to include Three Mills. We were already considering this as the potential headquarters of the National Fairground Museum. That proposal had been linked to the unsuccessful millennium bid.

The National Fairground Museum people signed up for Three Mills. Then, at the very last minute, they got a better offer from Northamptonshire. They went there, only to go bust later.

But local businessman Edwin Shirley was aware that when the Jubilee Line was improved, he would lose his yard at West Ham, and was waiting for somewhere else to put his trucks and his gear. He looked at those big warehouses in Three Mills and thought, 'I could set up rigs here, store lorries and equipment, and stage rehearsals.'

He set up a rig for Paul McCartney when Wings toured, and built the whole stage in one of the warehouses so they could rehearse. The rehearsals finished and McCartney went off on tour, but they were doing an album as well and they were looking for somewhere to shoot a video to promote the album. And they thought, 'well, we might as well do it here.'

They got a video director down and started shooting the video. One day, Steve Jacobs went down and said to the director, 'what would it take to turn this into a film studio then?' And the guy said, 'about 200 square yards of white paint. You've already got a secure, enclosed space and big warehouses of the right height. You don't need anything else. We would bring our own gear.'

Edwin Shirley replied, 'that's a good idea.' And he opened Three Mills Studios. It was all about getting things rolling in the Lea Valley.

Michael Owens:

> Commissioned by Sandra Hunt, former Assistant Chief Executive of Newham Council, the Arc of Opportunity presented a vision of the Lea Valley from Stratford to the Royal Docks as a focus for high quality new development of all kinds built around new waterfront locations — a new metropolitan development zone.

Sandra Hunt:

> It's difficult to think back to the days when we were first there in the mid 1990s, when Newham wasn't seen as being anywhere. That's certainly how it felt to me. It was just some backwater where nothing much was happening, and it was seen as iffy because it was the East End. Raising perceptions was crucial because we needed the investment. You've got to get people on side. You've got to get political support for the initiative. You've got to get money. You've got to get commitments. There's no point having a plan if you can't make it happen.
>
> Soon after I arrived at the Borough, Newham was planning to promote its development sites at MIPIM (Marché International des Professionnels d'Immobilier), the international property development event held in Cannes each year. The boards that had been prepared weren't strong enough and I acted quickly to get them changed. That became the launch of the Arc of Opportunity vision. Later, the Barcelona-based architects, MBM, led by David Mackie, were commissioned, following a design competition to develop the vision and strategy. We were very enthusiastic about him because he did seem to buy into the vision. And he translated it into something that could work. It was important that he did buy into the vision. He was the only one who really understood that we were trying to create somewhere different, on another level. We needed him to translate that

into a physical vision. But it was just a master plan, after all, and it then had to be sold. It did what was intended. We wanted to enshrine it in the local plan to give it status.

We put forward a strong vision about what the place could be, and that proved to be a major driver for pushing individual programmes of work. It also gave us a way of rejecting schemes that didn't fit with the vision. When anything came along that was completely off the wall and wasn't going to fit, we were able to say, 'that's not part of the ambition for the area.' There were always those types who wanted to come along and build the largest, cheapest hostel budget hotels on one of the most valuable sites. At that time, when there was an awful lot of what I considered crap coming along, we had to push all that away.

Within the area designated as the Arc of Opportunity, there were maybe 15 to 20 individual streams of work, all happening at the same time. We kept some bits of infrastructure, made links, promoted some sites as catalysts, created masterplans, and established vehicles to promote some key schemes. We included the Royal Docks because it was a question of having as many assets as possible. The Arc masterplan meant they were seen as a whole, though each one had a life of its own.

We tried to use whatever was available in a given area to stitch it together. For example, what you see in Canning Town today is very much a product of that early work. Canning Town was the focus for master-planning, trying to deliver the site assembly and create partnerships and development arrangements, all geared to getting various bits and pieces off the ground. We were simply looking for as many opportunities and as much money as we could. We'd got this framework and we knew broadly where we wanted it to go, and it was a question of what could come from government, the private sector or anywhere else.

Michael Owens:
> Sandra Hunt made a case to the Government for large-scale investment in land assembly in the Lower Lea to unlock the Arc of Opportunity, arguing that the public investment would ultimately be recouped when private investment in property development was unlocked.

Sandra Hunt:
> Many of the local projects, programmes and activities within the Arc had their own life. We would support them, looking for a strategic synthesis between chunks of work. That was quite difficult in local places like Canning Town and Stratford. The work was costly and time-consuming. It was a hard slog. Politicians found it tough because they wanted to see results, while we were asking them to buy into something that required long-term investment and a long-range view.
>
> There was a crescendo point of excitement and interest around the year 2000. Newham was awarded Council of the Year and became quite good at delivering large scale projects such as the public realm improvement of the Stratford station concourse and the emerging proposals for the development of the Stratford rail lands. They had teams and structures in place for the first time. This made it quite hectic, and other authorities were jealous of that. Newham was seen as a slick machine, selling great stories, with good staff delivering realistic programmes. It continued in that vein for about a year and a half.
>
> Later, in the years before the Olympic bid succeeded, it felt like that difficult and challenging agenda had exhausted itself. There was a desire to consolidate, take stock, take a breath. You've got to keep up the momentum for years and years if you're going to deliver a transformation. And as I say, politicians work to certain timescales.

Some of the politicians were very good in that respect. The profile had been raised to some extent, but there were a lot of people in authority who didn't necessarily share the vision. I always had trouble understanding why there wasn't more interest in the place. It took a long time. It's very frustrating when you start on what you think is an exciting concept and it takes so long to get the building blocks in place. If you could suddenly wave a magic wand, you'd create the Arc of Opportunity. If that had happened at that point, the story would be very different. But it didn't, because nobody was interested in putting money into it. And although Newham was quite well connected, it was still seen as some distance away. If we could have waved a magic wand, I'm sure Ian and I would have said that what we wanted were building blocks, extra transport ... It's not rocket science.

In many ways, I suppose it was just too ambitious really. You were talking about a transformation, and you weren't going to make it happen overnight, so perceptions had to change until some real money was made available for certain things. We made some progress, but it needed a big oomph. The Olympics gave it enough of a boost, but not in the way that was desperately wanted, in my view. Maybe now it's starting to deliver a bit more in line with our vision, for example with the university presence, reflected in the arrival of Loughborough University and Birkbeck on sites within the Olympic Park.

Vivienne Ramsey:

The Arc of Opportunity vision served a purpose. It got people talking. I don't think it delivered anything that wouldn't have happened anyway, but it was a way of articulating a vision and making it sexier, bouncier and glossier than any local plan could ever look. It had some mad ideas in it that you couldn't possibly implement, though, like the proposal to add a new stretch of canal to the waterway network.

Michael Owens:

While Newham were putting together and promoting their Arc of Opportunity at MIPIM for their east bank of the River Lea, in true Lea Valley-style Tower Hamlets were assembling their own separate vision for their west bank. But their approach was very different. It was far more bottom up, and community driven, and for the first time acknowledged the need for a unified strategy for the Valley as a whole.

Paul Brickell had left the world of science to take up a post with the Bromley by Bow Centre in Tower Hamlets, and also was elected as a councillor in Newham: roles in two organisations, one on the west and the other on the east bank of the Lea; one a groundbreaking but nonetheless small voluntary organisation and the other a large, powerful and increasingly confident Local Authority; perhaps living with these contradictions sharpened Paul's sense of the strategic opportunity that could transcend physical, administrative, cultural and organisational boundaries. Paul would go on to become the Chief Executive of the Leaside Regeneration Company before joining the London Legacy Development Corporation (LLDC), where he is still Executive Director for Regeneration and Community Partnerships.

Paul Brickell:

I was Professor of Molecular Haematology at University College London, and I was running a research group and a research department. I was long overdue for a sabbatical. We had refinanced the lab for another five years. We were doing well in what was going to be the research assessment in 2001. I planned a sabbatical, but not in science.

I had just moved back to East London, because I was born in Forest Gate near Stratford. I had moved away to go to university in 1975, then moved back again in 1994 and met Andrew Mawson, a minister and social entrepreneur, through a group of friends connected with his church at Bromley by Bow. I started volunteering at the Bromley by Bow Centre in 1995. That challenged a lot of my ideas about health and community. I started spending half a day a week working in their community care project. I did mosaics with people with physical disabilities. In 1995, I became a trustee and began to do more. As I got more involved, I began to question whether I wanted to stay in science.

Around 1998, various programmes — via the Government's SRB funding and backed by Tower Hamlets Council — were investing in the area. Bromley by Bow Centre managed to secure a tranche of this government funding. The housing company Poplar Housing and Regeneration Community Association, HARCA, had been set up, and a new organisation, Leaside Regeneration Ltd, was being set up by the Council and several local organisations.

Suddenly, from being the forgotten corner of Tower Hamlets, the Council now cared enough about it to invent these two organisations: Leaside and HARCA. We started talking with them about their physical regeneration proposals and thinking about how you might deliver on them with local people. I spent six weeks early in 1999 writing a piece with Poplar HARCA about the relationships between Bromley by Bow and HARCA, how we might work together around some shared values, and the benefits of working together.

The Canary Wharf development was in progress. Canary Wharf was born in an era of banners and shouting. Everyone hated each other and it was bruising. Nobody believed that Canary Wharf had anything to do with the local community or that it would benefit them. In those early days it didn't — because if that's the story you tell, then lo and behold, that's what happens. We had some ideas and we'd done some work on those three acres of land on our patch at Bromley by Bow, when we got an inkling of something else that was happening. We saw in HARCA and Leaside an opportunity. We began to lay out our thoughts and look at the benefits and opportunities. We started to think about the bigger picture.

It was as early as March or April 1999 when Andrew Mawson began to talk about Water City — a phrase he'd picked up from Reg Ward — and the idea of Eastminster, which Reg had put forward. At the same time, Sandra Hunt and Newham Council were developing the idea of the Arc of Opportunity. They'd included the Water City idea in their vision. We both nicked the idea off Reg Ward.

I was elected to Newham Council in May 1998, but I was very much on the outside. This was a language and a world I knew nothing about. I wasn't involved in the Newham plans for Lea Valley.

I completed my six-week sabbatical at Bromley by Bow and wrote the document in which we began to set out a broader context. We started arguing for a way of working that combined the stories of the direct involvement of local people in making change happen alongside large-scale ambitious visions. I went back to the lab and then about six months later, in 1999, they said, 'why don't you come and work with us as Director of Regeneration at Bromley by Bow?'

I started working in the Bromley by Bow Centre two or three days a week. Three years later, I became full-time. I can remember on my first day walking across to Three Mills to speak with the people from the River Lea Tidal Mill Trust and I was amazed at the space there. Three Mills made me think. We wrote about water and its ability to power the economy, and explored the idea of a new piece of the city with its own unique qualities based on water as terrain and as metaphor: the water of life; water as constantly flowing and renewing.

Michael Owens:
>I met Paul Brickell for the first time in 1998, not long after I had been appointed as Chief Executive of the Leaside Regeneration Company. I went over to meet Paul and Donald Findlay and said, 'there's a line in this regeneration programme about social enterprises and it's got Bromley by Bow's name against it.' We started writing about and developing those ideas. I picked up ideas on the theme of Water City from Paul and his colleagues. I began to work with Paul, playing with the metaphor and writing similar things in the context of Leaside, expressing proposals for projects in the context of Water City as an overarching strategic vision.
>
>The Leaside Board included Eric Reynolds from Trinity Buoy Wharf, Steve Stride from Poplar HARCA, Richard Brown from Docklands Light Rail, Richard Gooding from London City Airport, Andrew Mawson, and several other influential stakeholders. I think they were an extraordinary group of people from the inside and outside of various camps. They were excited and enthusiastic about this place. Civilisation hadn't quite discovered the Lower Lea Valley at that stage. But Reg Ward and Ralph Ward already understood something of its possibilities. Between us we started pulling that story together.

Paul Brickell:
>Officially, the Arc of Opportunity, led by London Borough of Newham, had traction and nothing else did. No one was prepared to conceptualise the area with the River Lea in the middle. Andrew Mawson and the group involved in Leaside Regeneration Company tried to promote the Water City brand because it stretched across borough boundaries and went beyond individual places like Canary Wharf and Old Stratford. They each had their part in the story, but no one was telling the whole story, which is what we were trying to do, I think.

Steve Stride was pushing the Neighbourhood Renewal Fund at the time. What we wanted to do was bring those two ideas together: community in the setting of a more expansive Lower Lea regeneration story. That was an unbeatable idea. Michael Owens was working through the night in the Leaside offices to pull the bid together, and I had gone with Andrew Mawson on a church weekend to Stanton Guildhouse. I took the papers with me and worked on them under candlelight. The others went off on a walk and I had a pile of these bloody things. I was sitting in the library surrounded by artefacts of Gandhi. Not all the officials wanted us to do it, but you and I actually wrote the bid while others were just talking about it. We won £21m (£20.7m actually — a number engraved on my heart!) of SRB funding and that gave us quite a platform to deliver projects.

Michael Owens:

All of that gave us the option to do quite a lot of things. Between 1999 and 2001, we developed the programme and wrote the Orange Book — the Leaside framework and vision. The Orange Book set out a programme for a twenty-year period. Leaside delivered some of that programme. Paul and I worked closely together on that vision and framework, supported by the partners on the Leaside Board.

Paul Brickell:

Later, we delivered some of the infrastructure with funds from other sources like the new London Thames Gateway Development Corporation (LTGDC) and more recently, the Housing Zone. Nobody ever said, 'that's stupid and we shouldn't do it' to anything in that framework and vision. The passage of time has shown the document to be entirely prescient and correct. And the bodies that ended up leading the regeneration programmes in the context of the Olympics always ended up delivering it, even though at the time the fact that we took it upon ourselves to write it was seen as impertinent.

Michael Owens:

At the start of 2002, I took up a new post in the London Development Agency (LDA). Paul Brickell was appointed as the new Chief Executive of the Leaside Regeneration Company and continued the work.

Paul Brickell:

I took over Leaside Regeneration Ltd and we scoped out a vision, which then became current. We produced some artwork which showed the Lower Lea as a single area straddling the borough boundaries. Again, the boroughs weren't keen, not really joined up. I don't know if anyone in the LDA thought it was a good idea. Newham didn't think it was a good idea. But I believe, and I'm happy to be challenged on this, that they were the first set of maps, the first economic framework in decades, to show the Lower Lea Valley as a whole. These days, showing a map of the whole area is commonplace, but at the time we first did it, the scions of London government were kicking and screaming — they thought it was impertinent of us to have a view about our place — we might have known our place but we 'didn't know our place'!

Michael Owens:

My experience inside the LDA was that before the Lea Valley became a political priority, there was a lot of freedom to shape ideas. As soon as the area became a priority, there was intense scrutiny and control from the centre.

II

Ralph Ward:
> Despite all the enthusiasm, development in the Lea Valley on any scale was always going to be a difficult and expensive proposition. The Valley was blighted by all manner of problematic infrastructure, criss-crossed by railways and waterways and overhead powerlines, and land ownership was in the hands of a myriad of owners. Piecemeal development was not going to achieve the kind of impact required to create the market confidence that would build momentum for change across the area. It was going to need billions, and no regeneration programme of the day was ever going to get close to finding that much money. This would require some special reason, some mega investment. An Olympics perhaps? But no one, even the most ambitious local voices, were going that far. No one, that is, except Richard Sumray.
>
> Richard Sumray was the Chief Executive of London International Sport, an organisation he founded in the 1990s dedicated to holding another Olympic Games in London. A London location, he maintained, was the only realistic hope of hosting another Olympics in the UK. And that location should be, of all places, East London, in order to reap the unique development rewards it offered. Back in the late 1990s, in local government and planning circles, Richard seemed to

be the only person talking with good humoured perseverance about sport in the context of the Lower Lea. Everywhere we went, there he was, championing the proposal for an Olympic Games in the Lower Lea to a bemused audience. For this, Paul Brickell calls him John the Baptist, wandering in the wilderness with the message.

Richard Sumray:

Well, I guess my story starts in the late 1980s, because I'd become Vice-Chair of the London Council of Sport and Recreation (LCSR), which was effectively the Sports Council in London. And in that role, I ended up chairing two groups, five years apart, that developed strategies for sports for London. In the late 1980s, I turned up at a board meeting slightly late, and they were already involved in a discussion about how to involve young people in sport. As I sat down, I said, off the top of my head without any thought whatsoever, 'bid for the Olympics.' I mean that is literally it.

At the time, I was also the chair of the Association of London Authorities (ALA) Arts and Recreation Committee. The ALA hosted a conference looking ten years ahead at what the whole picture would look like, towards 2000, and I proposed that we should focus on the possibility of hosting the Olympics. That conference got me into trouble, because at that point, Manchester was bidding for the 1996 Olympics. When Manchester lost that bid, I persuaded my senior colleagues in the London Council of Sports and Recreation to support a London bid for the 2000 Games. At the same time, Seb Coe decided to make a bid for the 2000 Games. Seb Coe's proposal was for a bid based on West London, while our proposal was to bid for a Games located in East London, because of the opportunities the Games would bring to regenerating the area. The British Olympic Association (BOA) said it would not accept more than one bid from London, and the parties agreed to join the proposals together. After long discussions, it was agreed that we would propose a bid based on East London. In 1991 we lost that case: the BOA decided to support Manchester's bid to host the 2000 Games. A couple of years later, I led a bid for London to host the 2002 Commonwealth Games and again lost to Manchester.

We turned our attention to the future. With the help of Andy Sutch, the Director of LCSR, we set the objective of bringing major sporting events to London, with a long term aim to host the Olympic and Paralympic Games here.

I maintained contact with the BOA and set about persuading them that only a London-based bid could realistically be a possible winner, because it was the only city in the country that was sufficiently well known to win an Olympic bid. I persuaded the BOA in the beginning of 1997 not to have a competition, but to select one city (London) for the UK bid. BOA Chairman Craig Reedie decided to host a dinner that I organised. This was attended by key London figures, who were briefed in advance and they assured him that London was serious about making that bid. It should be remembered that London had no Mayor and no strategic authority at the time. Nevertheless, the BOA decided to focus on London.

The BOA had decided not to bid for 2004, so it was a question of whether to bid for 2008. And that depended on who was going to win in 2004. If a European city was going to win in 2004, we weren't going to bid in 2008. In 1997, Athens won the right to hold the 2004 Games, so Craig (Reedie of the BOA) and I had a quick telephone call and agreed that we wouldn't bid for 2008. This gave us time to prepare for 2012, the earliest opportunity to make a bid.

I proposed to the BOA that we establish four working groups to develop a possible bid: the location of the athletes' village, the location of the stadium and other venues, transport and environment. I chaired all of them and many willing organisations joined them. The London Planning Advisory Committee led the work on the location of the village. It wasn't about proving a particular pre-selected location in London as the best at that point; it was important to assess all the options. But we felt strongly that if at all possible it should be based in East London, the most deprived part of the country and in dire need of regeneration. Our previous scheme developed back in 1990 for the 2000 bid had proposed a stadium at Silvertown in the Royal Docks, with part of the Olympic Village in Greenwich and another part out in Beckton. Silvertown was no longer feasible as the LDDC had subsequently developed the site for housing. From the mid-1990s for me the most important reason for hosting the Olympic Games was so that it could be the catalyst to regenerate East London.

We reviewed the scope for a bid based on East London, West London, or a mixture of the two. It quickly became apparent that a mixed bid was not feasible as the journey times for athletes would be too long. The problem then for an East London-based bid was that a new Wembley Stadium in West London had been designated as the National Athletics Stadium as well. It was never going to work with a village in East London and the main stadium in West London — competitors would have had significant advantages over London.

What changed was the design and capacity of the stadium. I discovered that the spectator capacity at Wembley wasn't enough for an Olympic Games. In football mode it was 80,000, but in athletics mode it was reduced to 57,000, which was not sufficient.

I had this exchange of letters with the Sports Council. 'Why have a 57,000 stadium for athletics if you're not going to host the Olympics? There's no point in that, so why have it? It's a waste of time!' I handed over the issue of the problematic design of the stadium to the BOA and let them run with it, because they could clearly conduct a discussion at a different level to me at that point. That led to the Department for Digital, Culture, Media and Sport commissioning a second group of architects to look at the stadium. This was in 1999. Their report said that there were significant problems in Wembley hosting athletics. Then, out of the blue, the Secretary of State, Chris Smith, announced in Parliament on 1st December 1999 that, after careful consideration on the grounds of practicality and value for money, it was not viable to host both athletics and football at Wembley, and that athletics would not be a part of the project.

I saw this as my opportunity to start working with the East London boroughs to see whether they would be interested in an East London-based bid. I set up two groups. The first was a group of senior officers from the local authorities to explore the possibilities. The second was a small group that met in architect Richard Rogers' practice, around 2001, to brainstorm what an Olympic Park in East London could look like. And from the latter came the concept of the Water City.

In the Village Working Group we looked at 50 potential sites across London, and then we explored 11 of them in greater detail. What came across, in the end, was the strength of two sites in Stratford: one area in Hackney Wick and another in Stratford. Why did we want East London? For me, it was about Stratford being the catalyst for regeneration. Thames Gateway looked to me to be struggling. Canary Wharf never made sense to me, not in terms of community regeneration anyway. It seemed to me that it was separated from what was happening in the rest of the world. What I absolutely wanted was a concept of regeneration that included local people being pivotal and key to it, rather than separated from it.

Notwithstanding this focus, the case still had to be won with the authorities that an East London bid was preferable to West London. I had gone back to Barcelona six months after their Games, and I saw their docks area transformed on an ongoing basis after their Games. It started to dawn on me that we could achieve something much more profound. West London, I felt, was already overheated. There was a lot going on there; all the growth was in the West London corridor. Nothing was really happening in East London other than Stratford, where good rail links were being developed. But it needed a major kickstart — and I always use that word 'kickstart' — and it always felt to me that a Stratford-based Olympic Games could be that kickstart. Nothing else could create that stimulus for national intervention.

Conor McAuley:
The idea of having big venues in the Borough and attracting people to Newham was, well, in our heads. The LDDC looked at the Royal Docks as a potential Olympics site at one stage in the mid 1990s. Then in 1995, when the Football Association were looking to build a new national sports stadium to replace Wembley, they looked at both Royal Docks and Stratford as an alternative to rebuilding Wembley, though that is what they eventually chose to do. It wasn't such a crazy idea, then, to host the Olympics in the East. We were supposed to host the World Athletics Championships at Lea Valley Park in 2005, to replace Wembley, which wasn't completed in time. That never happened, but we were always looking for some way of promoting the area. 'You could do it here. You could do it there.' And again, we were always pushing the idea of having big venues in the borough. Before the Dome got built, and before ExCeL got built, there was an American proposal for an O2-type venue on the ExCeL site. They got as far as seeking building regulations approval.

One of the recessions came and the money went away, so we got ExCeL instead, which is fair enough I suppose. But we could have had the O2, you know what I mean?

Paul Brickell:

Richard Sumray was the John the Baptist of the London 2012 Olympic Games. He was a lone voice — nobody else wanted it in the East. The Newham regeneration team absolutely did not want it. They saw it as a distraction from the main task of renewing Newham.

My Olympic story began when I was taking a sabbatical period from my academic position and working with Andrew Mawson at the Bromley by Bow Centre. Richard Sumray contacted Andrew Mawson, who knew architect Richard Rogers. Richard Rogers said, 'that's very exciting, I think we should do that.' Richard got his colleague Mike Davies involved. And so it grew.

Michael Owens:

Paul Brickell told me about the proposals and invited me to one of the workshops with architect Mike Davies at Richard Rogers' offices in Hammersmith. I got excited and we took a report to the Leaside Regeneration Board, who agreed to support the proposition.

Paul Brickell:

Meanwhile, Steve Jacobs also got excited and came along from the Newham side, where he was running Stratford Regeneration Partnership. Then a chap called Steven Lawrence got involved. Latterly, the people who took over leadership of the Games didn't exactly serve Richard Sumray's head on a platter, but they marginalised him terribly. They stuck Richard out in the cold. Richard should be honoured for the work he did in that role. If it were not for Mr Sumray, it wouldn't have happened. He got us really excited as a local community organisation. He went everywhere, and everywhere he went, he got people excited.

The understanding and the vision came partly from Newham — from Sandra Hunt and her work with MBM Architects on the Water City vision, and then with Roger Zogolovich on the land assembly and development proposals. Starting from there and working with their ideas, we asked, 'how do you see the bigger picture, in a geographical sense and in terms of a way of working — getting communities and business working? How do you weave communities into this, so they are the shapers, champions and beneficiaries of change instead of none of those?'

At that stage we were learning. I think we invented that thinking. We learned quite a lot from Bromley by Bow, and we stood on the shoulders of people like Reg Ward, who hadn't understood the community bit but who had understood the geography and the time.

We began to draw up plans for how the Olympics would be sited in the Lower Lea and to help make the Water City vision a reality. I remember talking about this with Hilary Armstrong, when she was the minister responsible for the Department of the Environment, Transport and the Regions, saying there was an opportunity to do something bigger: to marry up a single regeneration programme with a neighbourhood renewal programme. Leaside was part of a bigger regeneration initiative called Water City. And if we really played our cards right, we could win the 2012 Olympic Games and deliver Water City.

The idea of bidding for the Olympics in East London took root in a few community organisations, later in a few local authorities, and then the Greater London Authority. To make it real, it had to get into government, and that's when the people involved at the start begin to lose the story. It's correct to say that it got traction locally before it got traction in London and elsewhere, because that's documented with dates. What's interesting is the question — and I don't know the answer — of whether it would have got traction without that local traction. Was it important to the people who took it into central government to be able to say that it was all supported locally? How much of our story fed into their thinking? I don't know, and I'd like to know that.

Richard Sumray:

In 2000, London elected a Mayor (Ken Livingstone). I was going to Sydney (for the 2000 Olympics). I suggested and he agreed that I would represent him there. I had a phone discussion with Kate Hoey (then Minister for Sport) at the time, and it turned out she was in the same stadium as me in Sydney watching the same event! I was in touch with Kate, talking to the Government about a London Olympics, and trying to get Ken Livingstone's office interested. Because I was also on the Metropolitan Police Authority, I spent more of my time at that point in Romney House (the Mayor's initial office), and had access to his key senior advisers whom I tried to persuade to support an East London bid.

The Government decided they wanted a cost-benefit study, given the overspend on Manchester's Commonwealth Games. I offered to chair the work on this, with the DCMS, the British Olympic Association, London International Sport, the Mayor: all key stakeholders. We chose and Tony Winterbottom, Director at the LDA, commissioned Arup to carry out the work. I believe that study was paid for half by government, half by the LDA. Mark Bostock (Director at Arup) led the Arup team and the document they produced was a key step in the process that eventually led to the government adding its support to the bid for 2012.

Ralph Ward:
> We have already met Mark when he was responsible for planning and promoting the Channel Tunnel Rail Link route through Stratford. Mark is one of the key characters in our story. As Arup's chief economic planner and director, he played a leading role in weaving together ideas and plans for Stratford, Stratford City, the Lea Valley and the Olympics. He led the hugely influential feasibility study into the costs and benefits of hosting the 2012 Olympic Games in Stratford.

Mark Bostock:
> We were criticised for that piece of work, but I must remind people that we weren't allowed any field visits; we were asked to consider the costs and benefits of a specimen Games based in the Lower Lea Valley/Stratford. Although it wasn't real, it had to consider the issues. But one or two things came out of that which were hugely important: first, to identify from the outset the regeneration benefits which would arise from hosting the Games as the basis for establishing a legacy masterplan on which the Olympic overlay would be placed; second, to make sure that anything built has a long-term legacy. Some may blame me for advocating that the stadium should have been designed solely as an athletics stadium for its legacy use. That is correct. I did it on the very simple premise that London, as a metropolitan area and a major city in the world, needed to house proper sporting facilities in order to get the full benefit from hosting major events in future years, and Crystal Palace was not up to that. So I saw an athletics stadium — a proper one, to take national, regional and international events — as being the legacy use for the International Olympic Committee's 80,000 seater stadium specification. So, we proposed to start with the design for a modern athletic stadium seating 30/40,000, and then provide on a temporary basis the requirements specified for the Stadium. Football was

being well catered for by the new national Wembley Stadium which was under construction at the time.

When we were doing our work, which was a very short: a 16-week period I think, we had a very cynical government to deal with, represented by civil servants, all of whom were totally opposed to the concept of London hosting the Games. After we completed it, the Government sat on it for six months. There have been several recent books trying to piece together the politics and decision making process which led to the final government decision to support the Mayor of London's intention to submit to the International Olympic Committee (IOC) an application to host the Games.

As I reflect on my role there are two aspects on which I want to comment. The first, already mentioned in the context of my involvement in securing the Channel Tunnel Railway Line, was the unlikely relationship which developed between two Deputy Prime Ministers each from different political parties, and Arup. This was the reason for securing the Arup alignment for the high speed railway linking London with Europe. As with the Olympics, it was my Arup report on the costs and benefits of hosting the Games that brought together in the end two unlikely Labour party personalities, Tony Blair, the Prime Minister, and Ken Livingstone, the Mayor of London. This partnership was the pre-condition for the successful London bid to host the 2012 Olympic Games.

The second aspect was that whilst the Government was initially hostile to the concept of a Games being hosted in London, it also became very clear that Londoners were equally sceptical and did not believe their city had either the infrastructure or the capacity. This view was also held by the BBC. They commissioned me, a few days before the IOC evaluation team was to descend on the city to give them a professional view on whether the London bid was real and deliverable. My reporting involved five or six separate live interviews on BBC News24 at the various venues for Olympic sports done over a two day period. That was an experience in itself. Immediately following this they extended my contract to do the same in Paris. On our return to London my final live interview took place in the last Eurostar carriage. The BBC staff relocated the few passengers to other carriages. Once done, James Pearce, the BBC Sports commentator, walked down the aisle and said, 'well, Mark, it is unusual for the BBC to commission an independent view. Is it London or Paris?' My response was a summary of the technical aspects of each bid. 'No, Mark,' James interjected, 'which is the best technical bid?' I hesitated and said 'London'. James switched off the live feed and said, 'you have either made a mistake or you are the only person on this planet to say that London has a better bid that of Paris.'

During the feasibility study Martin Jones was our contact at the LDA, and that was our introduction to Gareth Blacker and Tony Winterbottom. They were a very powerful duo. The LDA had their own peculiar internal politics, but it has to be said that if the land assembly process hadn't started when it did, and hadn't been driven forward, then you wouldn't have had the Olympics.

Sandra Hunt at Newham Council had been working on the idea of the Arc of Opportunity, and Richard Rogers and Andrew Mawson were beginning to talk about Water City. We got involved with the concept of the Water City much further down the road, when the Olympic Development Authority (ODA) was set up and went out to tender for master-planning the whole proposed Olympic area. Andrew Mawson, Richard Rogers and others were in one consortium. We were in a different consortium, with Fosters. It was Arup and Fosters.

After we submitted the bid and weren't selected as the preferred master-planners, Andrew Mawson was very cross — as was I. We thought we had it in the bag. EDAW (international landscape architecture, urban and environmental design practice) won. In a way, we were quite pleased that we didn't get it because I think our proposition was probably closer to Andrew Mawson's than EDAW's. Produce a legacy masterplan first, and then put your Olympic overlay on that.

Anyway, I was pleased that they got it because it would have been difficult to manage and to deliver what we wanted to do. Forget what the client wanted; we wanted to get a legacy plan out first. The reason for that was my experience of Birmingham's bid for the Olympics in 1985. That taught me a huge amount about the way one does these things. It's to get the catalytic impact from the Olympic overlay sorted on a predetermined legacy masterplan. And if that is not done, you get some serious mistakes, one of which is the stadium.

Michael Owens:

Although Arup did not win the commission to deliver the master plan for the Olympic Park, Mark and his team continued to work with local partners on strategic propositions for the Lower Lea, developing ideas for how the Olympics could secure a legacy for East London.

Mark Bostock:

Andrew Mawson and I started talking. He took me down to Bow to show me all the development there, and I have to say I was very impressed. I was also hugely impressed by the Bromley by Bow Centre, in terms of its concept and delivery, and I met up with Paul Brickell, who I thought was an outstanding individual.

We had a clear view that the trigger for the catalytic effect of the Olympics should be to create in the whole area from Stratford down to Canary Wharf a tier-one university, which should include medicine. Here was a wonderful opportunity for King's College London, University College London (UCL) and Queen Mary University of London to sort out their portfolio investments, to create the next Bloomsbury. It had to have some emphasis on sport, because such facilities needed to be integrated into that development.

Paul Brickell and an Arup colleague of mine, Peter Gist, spent a lot of time interviewing local stakeholders, potential partners and supporters. The problem at the time was, who do we talk to? All the layers of structure made it impossible to know who made the decisions and I'm afraid that was an impediment to inward investment from the rest of London. That clarity has only now come about with the legacy development corporation with its wide remit.

I recall some discussion as to whether that remit should extend down the whole of the Lea Valley and I remember thinking that it should. I was an advocate of that. I thought it should be L-shaped, because then it could take in Docklands and the whole surrounding area.

The interesting challenge to me is the future of the legacy company and how it should reduce its public sector content. How does it further involve the private sector and in what form? I understand the thinking that led to the establishment of the London Legacy Development Company (LLDC) in 2012, replacing the Olympic Park Legacy Company (OPLC). I think that once their work is completed one will be able to put one's hand up to say this has been fantastic. The Olympics were a very important catalyst in getting the Lower Lea Valley off the ground and I do not think London would have hosted the 2012 Games had it not been for the Arup rail alignment linking London with Europe.

I also think the strategic idea of an Arc of Opportunity, first developed by Newham Council, was hugely important. It was the first time that Newham in particular saw this as a huge opportunity for development. It focused their minds and gave them a context in which to try something different. A whole lot of things came together to create something which might not have been perfect, but it happened. And it may have come at a huge cost, but where there's big development, there's huge benefit. And that reflects on London, and on the nation as a whole. I think it's fantastic.

Michael Owens:

With the arrival of the Mayor in 2000, work started in the GLA on a London Plan. This picked up the significance of the Lower Lea, which it defined as an Opportunity Area. The LDA was formed as part of the Mayoral Group of agencies and also London's equivalent of the nationwide family of regional development agencies. The LDA inherited the regeneration funding streams from central government and was now responsible for setting priorities for their investment. The LDA had set up a Lower Lea Matrix Group — a group of stakeholders that would help the LDA define its investment priorities for the area. I was working for Leaside before moving to the LDA to run the Matrix group.

There was an opportunity to extend the considerable technical work that had been undertaken by London Borough of Newham for the Arc of Opportunity, funding additional studies — undertaken by consultants ABROS and AMION — to include land in Tower Hamlets, Hackney, and Waltham Forest. But it was clear that the money available would make little impression on the scale of the investment required. An Olympics, on the other hand ... As the Olympic Bid gathered pace, it would overtake the work of the Matrix group.

As we have heard, Ken Livingstone, the Mayor, lobbied by Richard Sumray, took little convincing that a London Olympics bid was worth supporting. But his support was unambiguously on the condition that the bid would be focused on East London. It was a risk. Like other projects — Wembley, the millenium Dome, Picketts Lock, it could easily become a serious embarrassment. But he had confidence in his team and couldn't resist the opportunity to extract a huge sum from Gordon Brown's Treasury, who were prepared to underwrite the cost, subject to an expert cost-benefit assessment.

Neale Coleman and Eleanor Young were respectively Mayoral Olympic lead for both Ken Livingstone and Boris Johnson, and lead adviser to Ken Livingstone on planning and development. They outline how London's new Government rose to the challenge.

Eleanor Young:

We didn't know we were going to bid for the Olympics until 2001-2002. And of course, even when we'd decided to bid, we didn't know we were going to get it. I think it's wrong to say that the Mayor's Office didn't recognise the Lower Lea as a priority before the Olympic bid. Remember, we were putting the London plan together between 2000 and 2002, and we had already identified the Lower Lea as an opportunity area in the London plan. The Lower Lea was a priority before the Olympics started. You've got to remember that the Mayor had to take a considered view of things, but he didn't take his time about it. Within 18 months we had grasped the concept that the Lower Lea Valley was an important priority.

But it was dawning on us that it would take a hell of a lot of work. Sandra Hunt's Arc had a cost of something like £300m; that was the LDA's annual budget to invest in the whole of London. And to cover the Tower Hamlets side of the Lower Lea as well — because we were saying it had to cross the borders so it couldn't just be based in a single borough — we were looking at a cost of something like £400m. From where I was sitting, that was a deeply intractable problem.

The problem was, how would we have tackled it without the Olympics? Where would we have got the investment from?

We needed a Plan A and a Plan B to deal with the situation when we lost the bid. We needed the Opportunity Area Planning Framework (OAPF). The OAPF set out a scenario for the regeneration of the Lower Lea irrespective of the outcome of the bid to host the Games. We never got Newham to agree to the OAPF. I don't know what would have happened if we had lost!

That's why Ken said the Olympics had to be there. That's where we needed to spend the money. There's no other way in a million years we would have got the money out of the Government. Ken had said we would only do a bid for the Olympics if it was regeneration, and it wasn't Wembley. We commissioned the Arup report, to see if it was worth it. That was in 2003. Neale, Tony and I went to see Ken with the report, which said it would cost £2.3 billion and only break even. We all stood outside and Tony said, 'what do you think?' I said, 'I think it looks alright; I think we should bid.' Tony said, 'we've got to do it, haven't we?' And Neale said, 'we've got to do it.'

We went in, and Ken said, 'right, we're bidding.' There was no discussion weighing up the pros and cons, because Ken had obviously read the report; he was a detail guy. He said, 'Neale, you sort out the money.' And from then on Neale was in charge.

Paul Brickell:

We started doing a lot of collaborative work between the boroughs, developing the thinking for the Lower Lea. However, the LDA made it massively inclusive and invited everybody along. We suddenly had a group which consisted of boroughs, the LDA and a couple of key people from every agency on the planet. When the Olympics came along, and

it became important to the rest of the LDA and the GLA,
I remember saying at the time that it was a good job we were
now planning for the Olympics because at this rate of growth
we were going to need an Olympic Stadium for the meetings
alone. It's a classic thing — invite everyone in and do the
real work somewhere else. They effectively closed down the
Matrix group and took all its significance away.

Michael Owens:

Eleanor Fawcett was originally an officer in the GLA's
Architecture and Urbanism Unit and latterly a senior officer
within Legacy Company. She reflects on the early design
ambitions as conceived in the Mayor of London's offices, and
her work to hold onto key principles as new organisations and
actors arrived on the scene.

Eleanor Fawcett:

I started working in the Lower Lea Valley when I joined Mayor
Ken Livingstone's Architecture and Urbanism unit in 2003.
Initially my area of responsibility was the London Thames
Gateway north of the river: from Rainham to the Lower Lea
Valley. As I became more experienced and more senior, my
geographical area of responsibility shrank and shrank!

Allies and Morrison and EDAW were engaged to work
up the planning application and proposals to support the
Olympic bid. At that time, my own primary focus was on the
Opportunity Area Planning Framework for the Lower Lea
Valley, which I always describe as the document we were
going to publish when we lost the Olympic bid, so we had a
good news story for the morning after we lost.

I started off doing the drawings, working with Mark
Brearley, a senior officer in the GLA's architecture and
urbanism unit. I didn't really understand why everybody was
agonising so much over governance structures: we would

produce drawings and take them to various meetings and then we had to make changes. I spent ages doing organigram after organigram, diagram after diagram, drawing on the conversations happening at the time, trying to create a logic for what should happen in the Lea Valley. I was so new to that whole world of local government. In retrospect, I understand it completely.

The work towards the OAPF became a vehicle for a joined-up conversation: it facilitated cross-boundary talking. It was mostly impossible to get busy people to the table, but the deadline and the potential for investment meant we could get people involved in producing a joined-up strategy. For example, one key issue was to develop an approach to industrial land release with the GLA planners and the boroughs. I remember producing lots of drawings for various options. At the time I thought it was all very dry — nothing to do with urban design — but I quickly realised it was the most important issue we had to solve.

There were several people coming to the Lower Lea with a 'start again' approach. By contrast, we thought the Lower Lea was amazing, with its waterways and the wildness of it all, the people, the history, and the culture of the place. Mark Brearley and I trained at Cambridge, where the philosophy was to start with what was there: no matter how unlikely the context seemed, to find what was special about a place and build on it.

Mark Brearley paid great attention to detail. Somebody would be talking about something obscure, maybe a road junction, and Mark would be like, 'yeah, yeah, that's the bit where the stairs do that.' How did he know all that? I took a lot of time at the start walking around the Lower Lea Valley. Every weekend I dragged my boyfriend, now husband, down there, taking photos and exploring. I am so glad now of all that early wandering. All those early expeditions stood me in good stead for the years that followed. I often know the place better than most.

Michael Owens:

Gareth Blacker previously worked in English Partnerships and was transferred into the newly formed LDA at its inception. Reporting to LDA Director Tony Winterbottom, Gareth led the work to assemble land in the Lower Lea, firstly to support regeneration, and latterly to form the site for the Olympic Park.

Gareth Blacker:

We did start to look at the Arc of Opportunity stuff in English Partnerships, probably in 2000 when the London EP team went into LDA, but there was no strategy that covered the whole area. The only assets were in the Royal Docks. Stratford did feature but it was very bitty. We did some work with Steve Jacobs at Stratford Development Partnership; they had a little office building just outside the town centre. But the involvement was very small, maybe putting bits of gap funding into sites or into small bits of land assembly. More strategic thinking came off the back of the decision to bid for the Olympics. It would aid the bid if we could demonstrate blocks of land being assembled in 2002/2003.

Even then, I didn't think winning the bid was a serious outcome. What it did was to justify releasing money for land assembly. When any underspend looked likely in any area it was quite easy to go in, hoover it up and go and get some more. The rationale was to try and get the sites that could be strategic, like the Carpenters company land, along Carpenters Road, which was a big block of contaminated land, but a key site. The dog track on Waterden Road in Hackney Wick was another one. With control of that site, it wouldn't be a big step to start regeneration in those areas.

In supporting the Olympic bid, we were also spending the money on sites you didn't mind spending it on. Another was a reasonably good quality triangular industrial site owned and well managed by Hermes. For that site we simply paid an option fee, and it ended up being very good for the Olympics because we wouldn't have wanted to take it out at that time; you would have had to pay something like £30 million to buy it. By contrast, it was worth taking out Carpenters and the dog track, which needed regeneration even in a non-Olympic scenario. It was true to say that while the Olympics provided a focus for everybody and it was something around which everyone could rally, there was considerable scepticism about the idea that it was ever going to come through. All the way through, the fundamental rationale was regeneration.

One last point worth making on the Lea Valley is that there were probably other locations in London that others saw as maybe easier, or at least worth considering, as locations for the Games, purely on the basis of the Games themselves. Pretty early on Ken Livingstone took a view that it had to be East London, otherwise he wasn't going to sanction the Games. In the context that nobody expected to win, he was very clearly using that Olympics lever as a chance to target an area that was seen as a genuine regeneration priority and opportunity. Ken was being quite canny and ended up winning the thing as well.

Michael Owens:

At the LDA, I was given responsibility for developing an investment framework for the London Thames Gateway. This would provide the policy rationale to support the LDA's investment in land assembly, development and regeneration in the former dock areas of East and Southeast London. In practical terms, the LDA's land and property team, with staff from the former English Partnerships team now merged into the LDA, were already running well developed programmes with a strong strategic rationale. The new investment framework would support the case for further investment and, importantly, align the LDA's priorities with the emerging Mayor's London Plan, led by the GLA.

The Mayor of London's Architecture and Urbanism Unit (AUU) had been established to promote great architecture and urban design in policies and projects. The AUU was led by Richard Brown, previously private secretary to Mayor Ken Livingstone. Now, as manager of the Mayor's Architecture and Urbanism Unit. Richard and the AUU worked closely with the LDA and with the GLA's planners, ensuring that the Thames Gateway framework reflected good design principles and aligned successfully with the Mayor's planning and policy framework.

Mayor Ken Livingstone decided to support a London bid to host the 2012 Olympics, and Richard's involvement in the Olympic bid developed from that point in late 2002 onward.

Richard Brown:
> The UK had had a failed bid for Birmingham and a failed bid for Manchester, and it became increasingly clear that if we were to be successful, it had to be a London bid. We didn't think the International Olympics Committee would be interested in second cities in the UK. I think officials at DCMS understood this, and I think the BOA understood this. There was an informal loose consortium working up an indicative bidding proposal, including Andrew Mawson, Richard Rogers, Mark Bostock from Arup and Richard Sumray. Richard Sumray of London International Sport is an unsung hero because he developed the idea that a London bid should focus on East London, and then kept the idea of a London bid alive. He and that consortium were trying to push the idea of a London bid onto the incoming Mayor's agenda.

After some thinking, Mayor Ken Livingstone realised this could be good. He was a sceptic about sport. There was embarrassment around the bid for the World Athletics Championships in 2005 at Picketts Lock (After winning the bid to host the Championships, the Government realised that Wembley stadium would not be ready in time but also refused to pay for a new stadium in the Lea Valley Park above Tottenham. The International Athletics Federation refused to countenance moving the event to another UK city so the bid had to be reopened) The bid had basically collapsed, and early in Ken's period of office there were various people who were trying to get him to rescue the bid. I think he made entirely the right decision which was, 'no, this looks like a basket case, drop it, let it die quickly.' But the Olympics could be good; it could really force the Government's hand on some of the spending needed in East London. If we were going to do it, we had to be serious about doing it; we had to get some good people.

There was a long period of negotiation in 2002-2003, which was when I started getting involved, about how both the bid and the Games would be funded. And there was work commissioned from Arup: a feasibility study looking at potential sites in East London, including Stratford Marsh, as I think it was still called, and Three Mills. And that formed the basis of an agreement about who was going to pay for the bid. The cost was going to be split between the LDA and DCMS, because the LDA would do it for regeneration reasons and DCMS would do it for culture and sport-led reasons.

They also established an initial understanding about funding the delivery if we won. One of the things that the Mayor and the Government wanted to be very clear on before any bid was launched was who was going to pay for what. Originally, the Mayor wanted the Government to pay for more of the bid and more of the delivery, but I think in the end he said, 'I'll pick up the slack.'

Ralph Ward:

> Once the Mayor had made it clear in early 2003 that he would support the bid, planning the project began in earnest. Most of the load fell on the LDA. This work was led by Director of Development Tony Winterbottom. Tony is one of those key characters without whom London would not have managed to prepare a credible bid for the Games, let alone actually stage the Games themselves, though his efforts went largely unrewarded. He seemed unfazed by the challenges the Games presented. The LDA did have many of the skills required to undertake the kind of work involved, but the scale involved and the speed required still presented some vast and novel challenges, not least the largest Compulsory Purchase Order in UK history, and the undergrounding of several of London's most strategic powerlines which carried 25% of London's electricity supply. Nevertheless, Tony — and his team — got stuck straight in. James Graven was a consultant project manager working in the LDA, who in late 2002 found himself in the eye of the storm as the demands of the Olympic bid took off.

James Graven:

> I was originally brought into the London Development Agency (LDA) in early 2002 to provide project management support for the Wembley Stadium development. The LDA's Executive Director for Development, Tony Winterbottom, needed help to get the project to build an improved access to the new national football stadium up and running.
>
> After that, Tony retained me to support him with various Mayoral Thames Gateway regeneration initiatives he was fronting up for the LDA. I started that work in September 2002 and continued into the early part of 2003, at which point it became apparent that London was going to make a bid for the Olympic Games. Tony then diverted me to support him to develop the LDA's input to a potential bid.

At that time, the exact nature of that bid wasn't clear, although the LDA board had passed a resolution to provide support in capital and revenue terms for the bid. LDA, on behalf of the Mayor of London, was going to lead London's input to the London bid alongside DCMS. I was effectively Tony's day-to-day project manager.

The LDA had already commissioned Arup to undertake a feasibility study into the scope for hosting the Olympics in London, based on locating the Olympic Park in the Lower Lea Valley. I saw that report early in 2003. It was the starting point for taking the project forwards. The report drew several conclusions. There was a price in terms of the costs of infrastructure and regeneration, and there was a proposition for locating the Olympic Park in East London. It was a short, sharp piece of work but it started to take on a mythical status. Although its conclusions were heavily caveated, it provided the basis for subsequent decisions, though the actual scheme that was being costed for the Olympics and the bid bore no relation to the one in the Arup report. They were chalk and cheese, yet the cheese was priced on the basis of the chalk.

As Executive Director of the LDA, Tony Winterbottom was tasked by the Mayor to develop the Olympic feasibility work. Even though Tony was a development guy, he was effectively tasked with taking on board lots of the softer aspects of regeneration for this project: social regeneration, skills development, and so on. There were other directors of the LDA who were responsible for those areas of business and although others within the LDA executive team were involved, Tony was the person who took real ownership and accountability for making it all happen. Most other people tended to adopt a watching brief, not getting too close, maybe because they weren't sure which way it was going to go at that time. So Tony was very much the face of the LDA and the person who made things happen in his own style, within the

LDA and the GLA family and with external partners.

The LDA had the funding and the powers to develop the project but the LDA only had the legal power to pursue the Olympic bid insofar as it delivered urban regeneration, so the LDA support for the project had to be justified in terms of its regeneration outcomes. The board approved most things that were needed without too much opposition at that time. In early 2003, the LDA had only really existed for two and a half years, and it's probably fair to say that it was still finding its feet. It had been created by bolting together bits of previous agencies, and it had never had time to form, storm and norm, and do all the evolutionary development things that new organisations do.

So the LDA was not a slick machine; it carried baggage from its predecessor organisations. Tony Winterbottom's team, for example, mainly came from English Partnerships, and they had a style of working that had to be commercially discreet and sometimes confidential in nature, rather than open and collaborative. They were suited to working on schemes with private sector developers and weren't natural partners with local authorities. That could generate suspicion from the local authorities, as to the LDA's intent. Local boroughs always had a fear that the LDA was looking to take powers and responsibilities from them. As a result, the LDA would regularly — both at an executive level and a political level — come up against challenges over what it wanted to do and the way it went about things.

Michael Owens:

The LDA found itself in an interesting political position. It had to build new relationships with the boroughs, with the Government, and with the London Bid Company, a proudly private-sector led body, known as BidCo, notionally responsible for putting the bid together. BidCo were not immediately taken by the Regeneration schtick on which the Mayor's Games was based, though they soon came round.

James Graven:
Into this context, the Olympics came along: a high-paced, time-bound, very public project that landed on these boroughs without their permission. The boroughs themselves were considering how to deal with the world that was coming. I think they could see the upside, the good that would potentially come out of the Olympic proposals, but they saw a lot of pain and weren't naturally conditioned to deal with a project like this.

Effectively you had a lot of organisations, none of whom were properly equipped to deal with the pace and the challenges. The LDA had similar challenges with the central government. A lot of its communication with central government was channelled through the Government Office for London. GoL was perceived as a bit of a postbox for central government and it was never quite clear how GoL's authority sat alongside the mayor's. The whole business of London mayoralty and how it was delivered was far more immature than it is now. And we had only two years to get a bid in. All the boroughs and the local communities needed to accept this challenge.

You have to bear in mind there was a lot of existing regeneration work in this area led by others that had been progressing for several years. Partnerships had been formed and were starting to see benefits. Suddenly from left field came this great big project with its champions who were effectively saying, 'well, we can deliver the same benefits, but we can just do it quicker and differently, and here we come.'

The LDA really was caught between several bodies: central government, local government, several local boroughs and boroughs London-wide as the Olympic project had a responsibility to deliver benefits across the city as a whole.

Everybody could see their regeneration programmes being top-sliced, reduced and delayed to support the Olympics. There was a need to manage the hearts and minds of what was happening across London, as well as what was happening in the Lower Lea Valley. The focus on the Lower Lea Valley potentially threatened other parts of London.

Within the LDA itself, executive directors empowered with delivering those other programmes were not necessarily supportive of what Tony Winterbottom and his team were trying to do. It's fair to say that even within his own team there wasn't necessarily wholehearted support for the Olympic bid. A huge amount of land would have to be assembled by LDA: hundreds of acres, hundreds of businesses, hundreds of disaffected individuals and communities impacted. It would be a bloody process and I don't think all the development team really wanted to do that.

Michael Owens:

The Olympic regeneration narrative took hold, driven by the Mayor of London's commitment to making the bid, based on the rationale that it should deliver regeneration benefits and thereby had to be in East London.

James Graven:

Back in 2000 there were lots of studies, with Sebastian Coe and others involved, looking at the scope for a London bid centred on West London. A logical person looking at it from the outside-in might say, 'well, you're redeveloping Wembley stadium in West London — make that the Olympic Stadium. In Wembley you've got the transport links — centre your Olympics on that. Dead easy.'

I think it was quite brave of the Mayor to make it a condition of his support that it was going to be in East London. It was a big change in philosophy and thinking.

BidCo was set up with Barbara Cassani as its Chair in 2003, charged with mounting the London bid. It adopted the name 'London 2012' for itself. Though it was largely staffed by secondees from the private sector, it was effectively a public sector body because it was funded 50% by the LDA and 50% by government. Each provided £15m. BidCo had a multi-headed governance structure, with central government and the mayor effectively both overseeing it. However, it was trying to behave independently, not constrained by its owners, delivering a project which was meant to be in the national as well as the local interest. Add to that all the layers of public sector bodies around the edges, and you had a cocktail of confusion in terms of governance, who was doing what, and who was in charge. Keith Mills, who had formerly set up Air Miles, was appointed as Chief Executive. He brought a measured approach and a gravitas that allowed for more mature conversations.

There was a regular stakeholder group, which involved the British Olympic Association and all the main public sector bodies involved. You had several people with commercial private sector marketing focus appointed to senior positions; Mike Power, recruited as CEO, came from Proctor and Gamble. This resulted in friction between their culture and that of government bodies. There was a culture of mistrust of the public sector from the outset.

It suddenly dawned on BidCo that, blimey, this regeneration lark and the public sector people involved in it — who they didn't want to engage with — were onto something. I think there was a nirvana moment, particularly with the communications people like Jackie Brock-Doyle, who worked with Mike Lee, Director of Communications at BidCo and others, who suddenly realised the power of the messages attached to regeneration. While some people from the private sector might have had little appetite for or understanding of the public sector and how you make things work, the irony is that, of the 20-odd chapters in the Olympic bid book, the public sector had to write about 15 of them. You needed civil servants, and you needed London Government onside from the outset.

Ralph Ward:

Perhaps the critical element of the bidding process was the design of the Olympic Park. The project naturally attracted many of the country's top practices. To their shock and surprise the prize was won by the unglamorous EDAW, then working in Manchester, masterplanning the rebuild of the area damaged by the IRA bombing in 1996. The selection panel felt they were the practice best able to keep all the many interest groups engaged, particularly local communities, as proved to be the case.

James Graven:

In 2003, the initial master-planning for the Olympics was done to support the interim bid submission and to sow the seeds for the planning application which would be submitted in September 2004. We recognised back in February 2003 that for an Olympic bid to happen, we needed a more substantial master plan, given that the only substantive work to date was the initial Arup feasibility report. We needed a more comprehensive plan which would stand up to scrutiny and form a basis of costing and delivery in the bid, and everything else.

We started the procurement process around Easter 2003, invited applications, set up a master-planning reference group chaired by Neale Coleman and with various people on it, largely public sector but including Richard Sumray and various others.

On 31 July 2003, we held the bidder day for the master-planning shortlisted organisations, and EDAW's was the winning proposal. They included community engagement as part of their offer: Fluid, the community engagement specialists, were front and centre. The bid team clearly recognised the importance of speaking to local people, and that was very powerful. People like Neale Coleman and David Higgins had antennae for the challenges of change and major comprehensive regeneration delivery. They understood that you had to bring local people and local politics with you, and they had the experience of doing just that.

Neale Coleman:

I chaired a group called the masterplan reference group. The fundamental decision was the appointment of master-planners. Barbara Cassani chaired the meeting. David Higgins and Howard Bernstein were involved. It was a vital decision. Jason Prior and the EDAW team won the commission. The thing about EDAW was that they just got on and did the planning. Jason Prior led the EDAW team appointed in August 2003 to undertake the master-planning work to support the Olympic bid, and continued to support planning and implementation up to 2008, by which time the ODA was driving the development forward. Jason is an impressive individual, but he doesn't have a big ego. He inspired people, and he was able to communicate and engage with the ever-widening group of people that were by now becoming obsessed with the Lower Lea and the Olympics.

Jason Prior:

In 2003 we won the design competition, the only team without a superstar architect. We hadn't built a model. We went in with a single document containing three drawings, and we ended up getting appointed. I figured we were marked men from that point on really. We barrelled into a process; we met government; we got on well with the local authorities. We handled the public consultation meeting piece well, I think, and got everyone on board.

James Graven:

In late October 2003, there was a conference, an all-day meeting held at Three Mills Studios. There, symbolically, a lot of the regeneration leads stood up and said, 'we back this.' You know, from Greenwich or locally from Tower Hamlets. That was the first time I'd seen them publicly say, 'we get this, and we are supporting you all the way.' So they were on record at that point.

The LDA found itself in the thick of orchestrating the inputs to a huge marketing activity. London was selling an idea, and the LDA was very much part of putting flesh on that idea. It would have been quite easy for the LDA to lose sight of its real purpose: to support the bid insofar as it delivered economic development and urban regeneration. There were an awful lot of applications for funding from all parts of London, on the pretext that 'it'll be good for the bid'. By and large the LDA resisted most of that, I think, but a lot of noise was coming in from the sides.

Fundamentally the LDA's remit was to put in play a masterplan, securing consent for regeneration whether or not the Olympics happened. The planning consent ultimately took account of different scenarios: a plan for the development of the area if London lost the bid, a plan for developing the Olympic Park in the event of a winning bid, and finally, again in the event of a winning bid, a plan for the redevelopment of the area for legacy uses once the Games were over.

Jason Prior and the EDAW team got going straight away, but it was a challenging environment. There was a regular forum where all the boroughs would meet on a Thursday, normally at 7.30am, when they would get updates and Jason

Prior and EDAW would come along and present their findings. The audience was a mixture of politicians and executives; it was the main vehicle for engaging the boroughs. The process was motoring on and the juggernaut that was local government wasn't nimble or responsive enough to keep up with that pace. The meetings gave the boroughs' senior leads their only real touchpoint.

Whenever Jason and EDAW presented to boroughs or anyone else, they used regeneration language. A lot of architects would have started with a physical interpretation and follow on with the socio-economic stuff. Instead, they started from a socio-economic impact perspective, and then turned that into a spatial interpretation. They started, then, with the socio-economic footprint of the area and the historical challenges. They did it in a way that people understood, building up the story of why we were doing things in a certain way. Jason made it very welcoming and engaging. It was an acceptable way of getting difficult messages through to lots of the local politicians and their executives. He was a natural presenter, excellent at cutting through the cynicism and getting accepted, and he talked in the language of the people who were charged locally with regeneration matters.

I know there was Water City and other ideas about the regeneration of the Lea Valley. I think there was probably a perception in some quarters that there was lots of hobbyist stuff going on, lots of intervention in local areas because it was interesting and an intellectual challenge. There was a lot of change in the area, but it was happening at a pace that intellectual curiosity allowed. Whereas the Olympics, if it did one thing, it catalysed all the existing work and existing structures, lifted them up in the air and sent them landing back down. Suddenly there was this locus that allowed everything to land in a place where it started to make sense on a big scale for the first time. The Olympics made everyone sit up and take notice of the scale of opportunity for the first time. I think the EDAW work brought a sort of totality of the potential to the area.

Jason Prior:

We kept getting told, 'when your contract is up, you've got to reinterview.' We were staggered on a couple of occasions that we got reappointed. We got reappointed five times. I think they saw us as the people who had the story on the legacy and the plan, and that we could articulate it well. Even cab drivers were now telling me how the Olympics were going to work. You know you've crossed the Rubicon when a taxi driver says, 'ah, it's all about legacy, mate.'

James Graven:

In Autumn 2003, John Prescott, the Deputy Prime Minister, was given a presentation on the emerging ideas in the master plan. Jeff Jacobs from GLA went along. He had previously been Prescott's private secretary. The GLA and the LDA, supported by Jason Prior and EDAW, updated Prescott on what was being planned. Prescott had gone down for a sandwich. He came up and listened courteously and then, you could see, it dawned on him. There was a link with the Channel Tunnel Rail Link, which Prescott had championed. He had pushed to ensure that the route came into London via Stratford.

Suddenly, you saw the pennies fall over the floor when he realised that his station was now right next to the Olympics, and it was all linking together. At that point, I knew that the Office of the Deputy Prime Minister was going to be right behind this, because Prescott suddenly got it. He saw the upside. It was around the time when tensions were building within Government about who would pay for what, from which budget, and I think that was a big turning point, politically at least, in terms of the Government's acceptance of what was possible here, and how this could be a really good story. So that was important.

There was a January 2004 deadline for the London Mayor and central government to submit an interim bid document, a short narrative. The launch for that interim bid took place at the Royal Opera House in Covent Garden. Ken Livingstone and Tony Blair presented that event, launching it with a bit of fanfare, and the first submission was in.

At that stage the cat was out of the bag: London was in it. Despite their previously troubled political relationship, Tony Blair and Ken Livingstone were in complete unison in what they were saying, and they were head and shoulders above everyone else on the day. They were speaking from the heart, without notes, and very impressively, about why an Olympic bid was going to be fantastic for this part of London and the UK.

By May, the results of the interim bid had come through. London was fourth or fifth out of the number of cities, so it was clear that more was needed to be done to improve London's chances.

Ralph Ward:

As the bid was being prepared there seemed to be consistent support from both the public and press. This was probably underpinned by the regeneration narrative but also by the surprisingly modest cost. The initial cost estimate of £2.35 billion was still the generally quoted figure, even though the report on which it was based was not intended to be definitive or final in any way. But the figure had stuck in the public's mind, and seemingly in the mind of the Treasury who had given a commitment to underwrite the bid. The LDA had done a spectacular job. As the International Olympic Committee deadline approached, the path was clear to approve the submission of the bid.

James Graven:
> There was a figure in the public domain that the bid would cost £2.35 billion. That proved to be completely unrealistic and the figure was later revised to nearly £10 billion. A line could be argued that the funding required was £2.35 billion by arguing that the extra costs were connected to the regeneration of the area, But the lower figure was based on some heroic assumptions in the initial feasibility work: for example, that the Olympic Village would be entirely privately funded and that VAT was excluded from the quote.
>
> EDAW's master plan was based on more realistic appraisals of the challenging physical environment and the infrastructure costs. There was a dawning realisation that the scheme was now completely different to the one in the initial feasibility study and therefore the cost would be totally different.
>
> The bid process accelerated the LDA's land assembly in the Lea Valley. I wrote the business case for the Treasury Green Book appraisal for a £743 million pounds budget for the LDA to assemble the land necessary for the Games. The paper argued that the land assembly would deliver regeneration benefits in terms of jobs, homes, brownfield sites regenerated, and social impact on communities. That business case was approved around May 2003, giving the LDA permission to use existing funds plus top-sliced funds from its other programmes, creating a pot of money that would be entirely focused on assembling land. That was the root cause of tensions within the LDA executive. The LDA's internal challenge was that it had to redirect its other funding to this great big pot of money.

Ralph Ward:
> One of the questions that kept cropping up throughout the development of the Olympic project was 'who is in charge'.

Was it the Mayor? The Government? The BOA? Students doing their theses on London 2012 even today approach me in a forlorn attempt to secure an organogram demonstrating how responsibilities were structured. A particular feature of 2012 was the importance it placed on legacy. How was that going to be managed? Who was going to be in charge of that? Richard Brown, who had been closely involved in creating a number of public bodies and agencies, including the GLA and LDA, found himself in the thick of it again.

Richard Brown:

The bid was launched, and a small team was set up at Canary Wharf on the 50th floor, under the leadership of Barbara Cassani. At the time, there was a Plan A and a Plan B masterplan. The outfit was called London 2012 Limited. It was known as BidCo generally, and Seb Coe took over leadership from Cassani in May 2004. And people started doing the work on the master plan. In the meantime, I was doing work with a very bright person in DCMS, Helen MacNamara, on staging structures — the organisational arrangements for putting the Games on if we won.

At the core, you would have two organisations. Firstly, the ODA, a statutory, non-departmental body with planning powers, compulsory purchase powers, 100% publicly funded, which would build the infrastructure. Hugh Sumner of TfL did consider whether there should be a separate Olympic Transport Authority, which was something that they had in Sydney, but we decided it should be part of the same organisation, because we didn't see the point in having two separate organisations.

Secondly, there was the Organising Committee which would be a publicly owned private company. We were also very keen that the Organising Committee and the Delivery Authority should be located in the same building — as they had been at a fairly late stage in Sydney — to enable them to iron out any disputes about scope and budgets in person.

The founders and members of the Organising Committee would be the Mayor, the Government, and the BOA. The host city contract is formally signed by the local Mayor and the National Olympic Committee, of which the BOA is ours. The government technically didn't have a role, but we wanted to tie them in.

In addition, the LDA, the economic development arm of the Mayor of London, was needed to deliver the land assembly and remediation, partly because that needed to commence before the Games. And this would all be tied together by an Olympic Board of political-level people: ministers, mayor and the chair of BidCo/the London Organising Committee of the Olympic and Paralympic Games (LOCOG). That Board would be the place where any disputes or issues were to be resolved and it would hold the master programme.

Legacy was very important, but the legacy plans were always less well developed. We were going to set up a 'special purpose vehicle', to deliver legacy, and the Mayor committed some money to underwriting legacy in the bid document. And there was a bit of jockeying for position as to whether that special purpose vehicle would be the London Development Agency or Lea Valley Regional Park Authority or something else.

In spring 2005, I was seconded from GLA to DCMS, where I'd been saying to Neale (Coleman) and to Jeff (Jacobs) that we needed a transition team. Rightly or wrongly, they said, 'oh well, you're it then.' I don't think that was quite the answer I was looking for at the time, but that's how it ended up. I went over to DCMS, but I was theoretically jointly accountable. It worked fine because I knew Jeff and Neale well and had been working with them closely, but it was all a bit of a mish-mash. There was a very tight construction programme which needed to kick off early on things like the power lines project.

At that time, there was a masterplan reference group that was overseeing the developments of the master-planning work. We secured a very loose planning permission before the bid went in, at a choreographed meeting of the boroughs in September, with all sorts of conditions. But it was a planning permission, so we could put a tick in a box. Because that was one of the big risks; I think people looked at other examples of major British development projects like Terminal 5 and thought: British planning takes years.

The bid went in during November 2004. They gave permission for the Olympic and legacy plans at that stage. The narrative kept going: if we don't get the Olympics, we do have Plan B. And that also gave Tony Winterbottom of the LDA the justification he needed to go around opportunistically buying up pieces of land when they came vacant.

In February 2005, the Evaluation Commission came over. Tony Winterbottom made sure there were people driving bulldozers backwards and forwards, looking busy when they came. The whole rhetoric was that work had already started. So there was a little bit of theatre created by shifting piles of earth. And then their report came out, which was technically fine.

I think there were some in Government who felt — and it was certainly Mayor Ken Livingstone's point of view — that this was a way of getting money out of Government. Two specific things he got agreement on, which I don't think would have happened otherwise, were the East London Line extension, and the northern ticket hall at King's Cross. Like so many schemes, these were both on TfL's to-do list but had never quite gained Government approval. But when you put in a bid for the Olympics, there are three categories of transport infrastructure. There is 'in place', which is obviously stuff that's already built. There is 'committed', where the government has said it will do it. And there is 'proposed', which is an idea that someone has got, that would be nice to have: ambiguous things subject to final business cases. And the IOC weren't interested in those; for them, it's either happening, or it is approved and going to happen, or it is not.

The Government had to sign up to all these things, but many didn't think we would win. There were some in Government who felt that an honourable loss to Paris would be the best outcome.

James Graven:

By autumn 2003, the LDA was making its first purchases of land for the Olympics. There was other work that was carried on in 2004 to unlock the development of the site, including undergrounding the power lines. The very first site the LDA bought was Carpenters Road. The Aquatic Centre was placed on that location because it was the only guaranteed land that was available. There was a notion at the time that London would build a swimming pool irrespective of the Games. We would have had this mad situation if we hadn't won the Olympics, with a 50-metre pool potentially in the middle of an industrial estate. It was shown there on the master plan to demonstrate to the IOC not only that we had the land, but that we were already committed to the funding to show our serious support for sport and regeneration.

The stakeholder map was complicated, like spaghetti, really challenging.

Ralph Ward:

There was no stopping the process now. But of the several critical risks around which anxieties circled like vultures, uppermost was the need for the Olympic Park to have planning consent before the bid. And everybody knew, or thought they knew, how difficult, complicated and slow the British planning system was, particularly in a case where four separate and very different local authorities needed jointly to approve the same enormous project.

James Graven:
A must-win for the success of the Olympic bid was to secure planning consent. That would start to dispel international myths around London's complicated planning system and the UK's inability to deliver major infrastructure investment schemes. Given that the bid decision was to be made in July 2005, the IOC would visit in February 2005, and the bid itself would be submitted in October/November 2004. To be able to write into the bid that we had planning consent, we needed to have the consent in place by September 2004. That was the target, which meant that the EDAW initial master plan, which had been prepared around Christmas 2003, effectively had to be converted into a planning application at breakneck speed over six months. The local authorities would need to receive the application by July to determine it in September 2004. The focus through 2004 was the collation of that planning application, which EDAW pulled together. There were 20-odd boxes of papers. EDAW was the lead partner in a wide consortium of consultants who prepared the application.

In the normal course of events the planning application would have gone to four separate authorities: Newham, Waltham Forest, Hackney and Tower Hamlets. The decision was made to hold an extraordinary event, hosting the four planning committees concurrently in City Hall. GoL played a significant role in brokering that arrangement. The role of the Mayor in planning policy meant that he couldn't give consent, but he could decide to refuse. The boroughs and the Mayor were still working out their interrelationships in planning terms.

Orchestrated by the GLA, which worked with GoL, the event took place in City Hall, where they all met on the same day and each planning authority came to their own views. Newham reached a decision quickly. Waltham Forest had almighty trouble because of a political split. They worked until late in the evening, but they got there in the end. The scheme that secured approval on that evening would be adapted further. There must have been three applications at various times over the ensuing seven or eight years. But the bid could be submitted with the confidence that planning permission had been secured.

Commitments to major infrastructure works were also made to lend credibility to the bid. One good example was the scheme to extend the East London rail line. Funds were made available, to the credit of Mayor Ken Livingstone who secured central government commitment to fund the scheme, securing a direct link between East and South London. A commitment was made — whether the bid was won or lost — that it would happen.

The LDA prepared its strategy for a compulsory purchase order, to prove it could acquire the land at pace and take control of the land for the Olympic Park. BidCo had to get a whole suite of guarantees from lots of bodies, public bodies primarily, that they would commit to everything in the bid book: whether it was assembling land, funding projects, delivering infrastructure, cleaning up waterways or undergrounding power lines. Progress had to be seen to be made on undergrounding the power lines in particular, so that the authority to proceed was in place should the bid succeed.

The bid was finally submitted in November 2004, followed by the visit of the IOC to London in February 2005.

Thereafter, it was largely a matter of the LDA continuing to buy land and getting ready for business as usual, while BidCo focused on the Singapore visit in 2005 where the final decision was to be made.

On the 6th July 2005, the IOC awarded the 2012 Olympic Games to London.

III

Watched by television audiences around the world, Mr Rogge opened an envelope containing the winner's name and told the hushed ballroom of the Raffles city complex: 'The International Olympic Committee has the honour of announcing the games of the 30th Olympiad in 2012 are awarded to the city of London.'

The London delegates in the hall reacted ecstatically, leaping up and hugging one another. There was also jubilation in London's Trafalgar Square, where several hundred supporters of the bid had gathered and in Stratford, in the east of the city, near where the Games will be based in a massively regenerated Lower Lea Valley.

The Guardian newspaper, Wednesday 6 July 2005

Ralph Ward:
>The country seemed to hyperventilate when the Singapore decision was announced. Some of those who would be most directly involved in the actual delivery of the Games were rather more pensive. It is a lot easier to write a bid, where you can frankly say anything and get away with it, than deliver the event itself. The small group who had drawn this short straw had already wrapped the wet towels round their heads and were refocussing on the challenge to come when the horror of the London bombings hit the next day and removed any remaining glamour it might have had. This was going to be very serious. Difficult but critical tasks falling to the LDA had to start straightaway to meet the 2012 deadline. Central to these was land assembly and the undergrounding of the powerlines.

Conor McAuley:
>When we put the bid in and were waiting for the result, I remember standing at Meridian Square waiting for the result to be announced, thinking, 'I hope we don't win this.'

Michael Owens:
>I heard a story that one of the worst moments of Gareth Blacker's (LDA's lead officer on land assembly) career was when London won the bid at the meeting of the International Olympic Committee in Singapore on July 6th 2005, because he had assumed there was no way we would win, and suddenly, it was OH MY GOD.

Gareth Blacker:
>I must admit, the day that we won — just after we'd won, and everybody was going mad and there was that pub in Trafalgar Square — I went outside with everyone else and one or two were tearfully overcome with joy. For me it was more like, what the hell are we going to have to do in the next two years?

Eleanor Young:

> The day after London won the bid, Neale Coleman and LDA Director Tony Winterbottom went for a swim in a Singapore hotel pool. They got up with a hangover and went for a swim on the roof — there was a rooftop pool in the hotel. Neale and Tony were swimming up and down, and Tony was saying, 'oh God, we're going to have to do the power lines contract. What are we going to do?' And after they'd talked and got out of the pool, bombs went off in London: the city and its people suffered a series of appalling terrorist attacks.

James Graven:

> On the day when the bid came through, I phoned the team who were working on the business case for undergrounding the power lines. I had to say, 'keep writing' because they were about to put their pens down. Had the Olympics not been awarded to London they would have said, 'forget it, that's it, job done', because no one was going to do that job without the Olympics. That was the only way those power lines were coming down. The decision brought financial clarity to a head in government circles. You couldn't let a contract without financial cover, and there wasn't enough financial cover.

Richard Brown:

> Many in Government were certainly surprised about winning. And were certainly shocked by the guarantees that had been given. To bid, you had to have all sorts of signed guarantees: about building venues; about banning ambush marketing; about providing the quality of hotel rooms that IOC members are accustomed to, etc. BidCo argued that you had to give an unambiguous guarantee that you'd fund everything, otherwise the bid would be lost, and this was all about winning the bid. They got Gordon Brown, as Chancellor, to sign up to funding the works: an open-ended guarantee.

There was a bit of shock in Government when we won. As one guy from Partnerships UK put it to me a few days after the decision, 'you've got the Treasury in a complete spin here. They've got their main three options: to delay; to de-scope and to say no, and each one is closed off.'

James Graven:

The Treasury expected London to be gallant losers, but they got a win. They had effectively written a blank cheque in support of the bid. All those commitments and guarantees had to be delivered and there was no getting away from it. Everyone knew the £2.35 billion was a nonsense in that it was a hypothetical cost linked to a different scheme from the one submitted. In the bid development years, Pricewaterhouse-Cooper had been commissioned to look at what the real costs were, but their report was never published. Their estimate for all the elements of stadia and regeneration came to about £6–6.5 billion at that time.

The political fallout of not releasing costings was a problem for another day. That day arrived when the bid was won. Between 2005 and effectively the end of 2006, the real budget had to be sorted out. Project Raven was set up to flush out the real numbers, and KPMG were appointed by DCMS and central government to undertake the work.

Neale Coleman:

Gordon Brown had said, 'there will be no Exchequer money.' We had to find some way of saying it would be cheap enough. Of course, you can play with any numbers from the Arup report (the feasibility study into viability of developing the Olympic Park in the Lower Lea) to make it say what you want, to show there would be no Exchequer money coming in. But we were in a very difficult position because it became clear that we hadn't got anything like enough money. There was a process of reviewing the bid, and the whole review process with the Treasury went on and on. We didn't know when we would get it fixed, and Brown — to his credit, I think, and contrary to the line Ken was pushing and I was supporting — added a very big contingency which took it to £9.3 billion. This required a whole load of Exchequer money to be put in — around £5 billion. That's when we put in £350 million. We were forced to do that, and we agreed to it. Ken decided we were just going to borrow it. It was a difficult time, and it took far too long.

Ralph Ward:
Assembling the site for the Olympic Park was going to require the largest Compulsory Purchase Order the UK had ever seen. Functioning businesses needed to be bought out, paradoxically on the grounds that this would be regenerative. Gareth Blacker and his team had cleverly already got several important land acquisitions under their belts on the basis that, come what may, they could be justified for the regeneration of the Lea Valley. But this still left several hundred interests still to be acquired, and alternative locations to be found or built for many businesses. The LDA's core purpose, after all, was to preserve and grow businesses, not close them down. In addition, the site of Clays Lane Housing Cooperative had been earmarked for the Park, as had some of the most beautiful allotments in London, and these were unlikely to go quietly.

Neale Coleman:
The Olympic Development Authority arrived on site in late 2008 and finished the development of the Olympic Park in 2011. You can see that in 2005 we really didn't have much time to hand the cleared site over to the ODA. We'd already got the power-lines project on site in 2005. That was a nightmare. The London Development Agency had to let the contract. That was

a very complicated contract, led by Tony Winterbottom at the LDA. We were doing the undergrounding of the power lines and we discovered that we didn't own one of the pieces of land. We decided we just had to carry on, and we did.

We were trying to sort out the land assembly and we agonised over whether we needed another planning consent for the CPO inquiry. We had to buy all these relocation sites in Beckton, and we did keep most of the good businesses. They were relocated. We saved many jobs and created new ones. For a lot of those businesses, it was the best thing that ever happened to them because they got a real benefit from their move into new premises. But that was a very difficult process.

At the same time, we had three lots of Travellers, three bus garages, the Kingsway International Christian Centre (a large and fast growing Pentacostal Church) and Clays Lane Housing Cooperative: the whole thing was a nightmare. The CPO inquiry was in 2006 or 2007. We got on site and the site was cleared by 2008. To get from the bid decision in 2005, when nobody thought we would win, to doing a CPO, taking it through inquiry, doing all the private treaty deals, clearing the whole site, and sorting out the bus garages and relocating the Travellers, all by mid-2008, which was when the ODA needed to be on site, was an amazing achievement.

Gareth (Blacker, of the LDA) assembled the land. Nobody had bothered to think in all the budget discussions about how the land would be paid for. The notion was that the LDA would do it through Prudential Borrowing. I'm not sure how prudent any of it was. It was a phenomenally good job that they did though.

Gareth Blacker:
Once the bid was won, we had to accelerate the land assembly so we could pass the site for the Olympic Park over to the ODA. It was critical that all that groundwork had been

done and the planning consents had been obtained for the relocation sites. We had to manoeuvre things quickly. We had to build buildings for people to move into, both bespoke and speculative, pretty much immediately after the decision to give the Games to London in 2005. Big sheds don't take long to build, but across all the sites we needed more than a million square feet of new industrial space for occupiers to move from the Olympic Park.

It was a big exercise involving many teams within the LDA — not just the development team, but the regeneration and business support teams. Every business within what would ultimately become the Olympic Park area was identified, and each was allocated a 'case worker', who took forward all the information about the company's requirements, their market area and where they needed to be relocated. All that was brought together. Then sites were found from existing LDA land in the eastern part of the Royal Docks, and new sites up in Walthamstow were secured to build new industrial estates. Other sites — transitional sites down in Silvertown for the waste businesses, and so on — were put in place. New industrial estates were built with development partners or land created for some of the bigger occupiers to do their own bespoke development.

The vast bulk of the dialogue with businesses was quite pragmatic. But I think they had a bit of a shock when the bid came through and realised that they were going to have to engage quickly to put in motion the plans that we'd been working with them on. There were pockets of hostility. Lance Forman stirred up more column inches and TV coverage; he played a good game and you can't fault him for that. (Lance Forman ran H Forman and Son, who had been curing and smoking fish in the East End for leading retailers and restaurants since 1905. It was a very successful business and he did not want to move). It was probably not the businesses but the other occupiers who were the challenging ones: relocating Travellers and coming up with a deal with the Clays Lane Housing Cooperative. They were upset and it was difficult. Everyone had their go in 2007, during the judicial review of the decision. The allotment guys were in the High Court. Belgian journalists who came over to cover it found us sitting there having a chat with them, which disappointed them terribly.

It was fraught and tense at times, but the whole thing was worked through in the inquiry. Over four months, every challenge that came in was met, with us working round the clock dealing with objections. David M H Rose, the Planning Inspector appointed by the Secretary of State for Trade and Industry to lead the inquiry, went out of his way to allow objections: he kept it moving, but at the same time he gave everyone an opportunity if they needed a bit more time. He extended and extended the inquiry, but he didn't allow big adjournments. He was very good at managing the process.

Ralph Ward:

The Olympic Park, probably the biggest development project in the UK, sat right alongside the second biggest, Stratford City. The logistics involved in developing all this simultaneously was problematic enough, but also because Stratford City provided the main route into the Olympic Park. Unless the shopping centre was complete before the Games, Olympic visitors might have to reach it walking through a building site.

Stratford City and the Olympic Park, despite being side by side, were being independently designed, really for quite rational reasons. Neither could be certain that the other was going to happen. The International Olympic Committee's perception was that unless the two projects explicitly worked together, and supported one another, they didn't believe that London could deliver the Olympics within the timescale because it looked too complicated. When this cooperation seemed to the LDA to be at risk they decided they had to add Stratford City to the CPO to guarantee an Olympic compliant outcome. Were the LDA seriously going to attempt to CPO the biggest commercial investment in East London, offering thousands of new jobs, on regeneration grounds? It all started to get very difficult, if not downright bizarre. Some urgent diplomacy was required.

Vivienne Ramsey:

London and Continental Railways Ltd were concerned about the position of the Olympics. Effectively, it threw all their cost planning and development assumptions up in the air. While we (Newham) wanted the Olympics as much as the Government did, we had reservations about what we would be left with post Games, and how the Olympics might change the development plan for the site. The ODA, the body set up by the Government to create the Olympic Park as the stage for the Games, were putting a brave face on it, but the whole time they were really worried either that Westfield wouldn't start, or that if it did start, it wouldn't be finished in time.

Gareth Blacker:

The most difficult issue in assembling the site was conflict over the land held by LCR and the developers of the Stratford Rail Lands. With the Olympic bid won, they got very twitchy because their land was in the CPO and there was a danger that they might get shifted out. They became quite defensive very quickly and worked out a strategy showing that only little bits of their land were needed to create the Olympic Park.

The position we took, and Ken Livingstone was quite strong on it at the time, was that we had to have certainty.

Either all the rights had to be formally signed up to in binding documentation, or the land had to be in the CPO because otherwise it would jeopardise the whole case. You had to have the certainty that you could get all the necessary connections from the Stratford station through to the site.

There were eight or nine days' worth of negotiations — several times through the night — to reach a settlement with all parties. It was the Thursday night before Ireland played the All Blacks in 2005 — I was going to Dublin the next day. We were up through the night. I went back to Dublin and ended up falling asleep.

The inquiry into the Application by the London Development Agency for Confirmation of the London Development Agency's 2005 Compulsory Purchase Order for the land in the Lower Lea Valley for Olympic and Legacy uses ran from May to August 2006. After the inquiry settled, there were still lots of details to be worked out with people, the logistics of moving all 200 businesses, focusing on practical issues involved in physically moving people and negotiating their compensation packages. It was all building up to the target date of handing over the site to the ODA in July 2007. It was very customer-focused, so they wouldn't have any excuse for not moving when the day came. The police said they were expecting a whole number of public disorder incidents. We had some rehearsals, and the police had a lot of 'what if' scenarios. They had their own command structure and civilian command as well. Up until the beginning of July, we had a big contingent of police on motorbikes, and the sheriff's office brought in lots of extra staff because they were expecting to be forcibly moving people on.

In the end, the whole month went smoothly. Nobody was evicted. Lance Forman was the last one to leave. We handed over the site to the ODA and the site was sealed, but he stayed on, and he and his staff were escorted in and out each day while he finished his new building. No one wanted the bad publicity, and we could work around him for a few weeks. The sheriff was very disappointed. The police got bored after a couple of days.

Ralph Ward:
> The success of the Olympic bid meant that those commitments and guarantees written into the bid submission, which had been backed by the Government, had to be delivered. A number of external appointments were made to augment London's delivery capacity, replacing conventional civil servants with highly experienced project managers, including Jeremy Beeton as head of the Government Olympic Executive. A 'shadow' ODA was created inside the LDA, pending the creation of permanent arrangements to begin the process of building the Olympic Park. The London Organising Committee of the Olympic and Paralympic Games (LOCOG) would organise the Games themselves. These were very different organisations. LOCOG was structured as a private company limited by guarantee. The ODA was public sector funded and accountable, set up by the Government with an unusual mix of development and planning powers. Once again Richard Brown was called upon to help put the organisational arrangements together.

James Graven:
> In the months following July 2005, arrangements were made to put in place a delivery organisation. Alison Nimmo, previously of the regeneration company Sheffield One, had been engaged in late 2003. During the bid process she was the conduit between BidCo and the public sector. She oversaw the planning responses to everything for BidCo. The International Olympic Committee regulations determined the governance architecture for the Games — requiring the creation of an

Olympic development authority to develop the Olympic Park and create the stage for the Games, and separately the creation of the LOCOG to deliver the Games themselves.

Richard Brown:

The transition arrangements were that BidCo would transmogrify into the organising committee of the Olympic Games. I think that worked out alright. At the time we were worried that there were going to be too many people whose job was doing bids but not staging events. Very few people from the bid period had that experience. The LDA took responsibility for doing early works in advance of the ODA's existence, acting as the interim ODA, led by Alison Nimmo. It was a bit tricky, and the contract for burying the power lines had to go out that way.

We also briefed headhunters to look for a chief executive and chair for both ODA and the LOCOG. I posted the letters for the appointment of the ODA head-hunters on July 6th, the day we won the bid. I went back to the office after I'd had a few drinks and swayed a bit as I put them in the post. I know that David Higgins and Jack Lemley were both appointed by the end of December 2005 because they came to the LDA offices just before Christmas. In spring 2006, we moved into the Canary Wharf offices and agreed the deal that these would become shared offices between ODA and LOCOG. It was difficult because we were having to satisfy LOCOG's desire for prestigious office space with our need to build a business case for public sector investment, which implied modest accommodation. In the end, a deal was done. The ODA secured planning powers later in 2006.

Jason Prior:

There was a period — a fallow period — for about a year after getting the Games in 2005 when we (EDAW) basically ran with it because there was no one else running with it. We were briefing people who were yet to be appointed. The budgets were being torn apart, but we were still going through planning and doing consultation. I said to my colleague Bill Hanway at the time, 'you know what? We're way too far out in front of this, you know'.

James Graven:

Everyone was very focused on 2012, but few were looking beyond that date. What was the long-term impact? That had been at the heart of the original vision. The regeneration of East London was always one of the first things that would trip off a politician's tongue. Between 2005 and 2008, ownership of the wider regeneration agenda seemed to fall away. The LDA had positioned itself as the guardian of the regeneration and legacy agenda for the Games: skills, employment, volunteering, and all those people-facing things. A team was established. Although the officers were highly skilled and experienced, the organisational context and ownership of their work was not clear. From 2005 through to 2007, the legacy agenda fell between the LDA and the emerging ODA. By late 2007, the ODA was firmly focused on planning, design and construction, while the LDA's land team drove forward the land assembly programme.

Richard Brown:

When the bid was won, we were still at quite an early stage in the consideration of legacy issues. I said to Alison Nimmo, 'shouldn't your job, or my job, or someone's job have legacy in the title?' And she said, 'I think it's really dangerous for anyone to have legacy in their job title because it means everyone else will think legacy is not their concern.' I think that's a fair point. I tried to set up something when I was working for her, a venues legacy group which would bring together people like the British Olympic Association, Lea Valley Regional Park Authority and Sport England to try and act as a client voice to understand legacy and ask necessary questions such as 'where are we in the programme of designing and building the venues?' and 'what's the legacy going to be?'

I was only at the ODA until late 2006. In 2007 after I left, the ODA got planning permission for their revised masterplan. And I think one of the conditions of this was that there should be a legacy masterplan framework. They merely did a Games and transformation (ie, the immediate post-Games period) planning application, which was cleaner in many ways than the LDA's planning permission, but it did require the preparation of a legacy masterplan. This was commissioned in 2008.

There was also a discussion about getting someone in to be a senior legacy champion. Tom Russell was in the frame because we knew what he had done in Manchester where he had led regeneration after the Commonwealth Games. He was appointed to the London Development Agency at the end of 2007. Tom's job was always to set up something that would ultimately split apart from the LDA, though there were many people in the LDA who wanted to hang on to the Olympic legacy. I joined the LDA in July 2008, largely attracted to working for Tom Russell, who brought huge experience of urban regeneration from Manchester and had been recently appointed by the LDA to lead on Olympic Legacy. I was also keen to work with Gareth Blacker, who was leading the land assembly process within the LDA.

The directorate included a land and regeneration team and a programme office, which was me and senior LDA officer Isobel Leavis. The idea was that the directorate would become a company, and these people would be the directors of the new organisation on an urban regeneration company model. We wanted to set it up in 2009 well before the Games, and I worked closely on plans for this new organisation with Andrew Gaskell, a hugely talented surveyor who sadly died of motor neurone disease in 2013. We did go on to set up the Olympic Park Legacy Company (OPLC) in 2009, and I'm slightly surprised we achieved that because so many people tried to stop it.

The original Olympic Board structure for high-level dispute resolution trundled on, supplemented after 2007 by a new structure called the Olympic Park Regeneration Steering Group (OPRSG), set up because the Olympic Board didn't have local politicians on it. The OPRSG also had slightly different government departments. The Department for Communities and Local Government was on it, and I think the DCLG and the Mayor led it jointly. DCMS were on it but in a slightly subsidiary role. The mayors and leaders of the Olympic Park boroughs were on it. And I think Lea Valley Regional Park Authority (LVRPA) sent members as well. It was an expression of the political consensus. It was established to oversee the development of the legacy master plan and the establishment of this new legacy body.

Underneath the political structures there was a shifting range of officer working groups. I used to be a bit naïve about this — I used to think that the point of political groups was to make decisions, but of course they don't. They represent the deadline by which time you must reach consensus — or do a deal — otherwise the issue will have to be discussed, and no one wants to have a discussion. The meeting is a celebration of a decision already made. I think that that's the law governing how bureaucracies work.

All these things grew like topsy. It's the law of bureaucratic life. There was an Olympic Board Steering Group and an Olympic Park Senior Officer Group. It became a meeting of 15 people, with three people from each borough and representatives from each governmental department, at which point you could no longer have a sensible discussion. So senior people started having separate meetings to get the business sorted out in advance, but others started turning up to those, and the cycle started again.

At the same time, the leaders and mayors of the boroughs around the Olympic Park had started meeting, partly to work with us on a strategic regeneration framework to achieve socio-economic aims, including convergence between this area of East London and the London average. The four host boroughs organised themselves into a body, then grew to become five host boroughs, and then six host boroughs.

Ralph Ward:

The Olympic project soon became a giant, professionalised slightly alien process which threatened to exclude local people. But local politicians and many sections of the public remained on board, helped by the approaches adopted by both LDA and ODA, who recognised early on that maintaining good relations was probably their key risk management tool to keep to their tight timetable.

Paul Brickell:

For some years, local players in the Lea Valley had been working to develop a strategic vision. Then something happened. The bigger narrative got taken away from us. It went to the big boys and girls in the form of the LDA, ODA and LOCOG. We knew at the time that this would happen, but that it would come back to us later. I think we invented the programme and we then lost control of the programme but thought about what we could do in the meantime, in the knowledge that what we did in the meantime would be important. And the programme would come back to us in the end, and the big boys would get bored and leave. But you need the big boys to come in; you need their money and their expertise, and you need that drive. There's a bunch of people who have access to the money and expertise, but it will come back to us. It is our job at the end of the day, and it will come back to us.

That's why I tell the story that way. We articulated the fact that getting the Olympics would provide the public and private sector investment that the area so badly needed, and put us on the map. We talked about whether we were going to get the Games, and whether the momentum above all this would be the thing that moved this area on from Canary Wharf. We drew on all the lessons, the Bromley by Bow Centre, HARCA and Leaside, to develop a way of working that wove social and economic regeneration through physical development.

We'd already started doing it, so we knew it worked. The Olympics was going to allow us to say to local people, 'change is not a threat; change is an opportunity. Go and get the skills, start the business, go into school.' During the bid phase, we said we wanted a legacy from the bid, and it was going to be all about getting people engaged and excited about change, about the experience and the excitement of regeneration. People said to me, 'We mustn't do that because we'll lose the bid and then people will be disappointed.' Then we won the bid. I mainly worked at that approach in my role as a councillor in Newham.

In Newham we had this massive Olympic programme, which started off with a big summer festival in February 2006. We hired a massive space and said, 'if you're in Newham — you might be a community group, a business, a school or a group of residents — come and tell us why winning the Olympics will make a difference to you.' It wasn't a show put on by the Council; it was a show put on by Newham. All these stalls were there. It was a cold Sunday morning in February, and I can remember we wanted to say, 'yes, the Olympics is a big thing. It's going to come in and take our powers and our land away. The big boys and girls are coming in, but that doesn't mean we can't shape it. Not by lobbying and shouting but when the Park is open and it comes back.' We needed the community to take the opportunity and not turn it away.

Robin Wales, Mayor of Newham, and I stood outside. You know when you've thrown a party and nobody turns up and it's a complete disaster? 35,000 people turned up. 35,000 people! After that, we invested heavily in volunteering, not just with the events but with everything. We had massive increases in volunteering and young people's participation in sports, and many other areas.

Another part of the story of that period is that universities began to engage and make plans. Birkbeck and UCL schlepped up. And the ODA was very good at engaging with people. We did the View Tube (a temporary building fabricated from shipping containers and overlooking the Olympic Park, housing a cafe and mixed-use spaces in 2009), which Jerome Frost commissioned. We, the politicians in Newham and my network at Leaside, were relentlessly positive about the ODA. We knew that the leadership required us to tell a positive story and we never really complained about stuff that went wrong. After the first year, we were relentlessly positive. We knew that this needed to be a positive story.

Neale Coleman sometimes gets bad press, but I think Neale really got it. Neale was a major force in creating the conditions within which you could run an Olympic project, bringing in people with substantial experience of delivering projects at that scale, like David Higgins. I don't know how to move four squillion tons of earth, so I think it was essential that Neale created the organisational infrastructure for that to happen. He and I would occasionally meet and talk about things. I remember one time starting a row with Neale. I remember at the beginning having a go at him about the green space and the waterways, probably for about a year in the early stages of planning, when we were trying to beat our way into this thing. I think Neale in his heart wanted all the things we asked of him. We came to an accommodation. And I think Neale might have a similar narrative.

Alison Trimble was at the Bromley by Bow Centre, a key figure in a leading local organisation in the neighbourhoods near to the Park, who helped set the early agenda. Alison explained it this way: Sometimes you need to be in tight control of the direction; at other times it's okay to adopt a looser approach. At that point we decided we didn't need to be in tight control of the Olympics. It would be delivered by big guns, but we were confident that in the long term, the agenda — setting the long-term future of the area — would come back to us. We decided to focus on those things we could control in the short term — mindful of the fact that when the show was over, we would be the long-term guardians of the area.

Ralph Ward:

In May 2008, Boris Johnson was elected Mayor of London. The change of Mayor well into the project had little impact on the Olympic Park development which was by now set in stone but had consequences for legacy. It signalled the end of the LDA, and some senior officers, ironic given the LDA's sterling work on Olympic land assembly. Their local training and employment had been exemplary as well. Legacy planning was taken over first by a company jointly owned by the Mayor and Government, before the Mayor elected to create a Mayoral Urban Development Corporation in his sole control. The Government, which despite its 'promises', couldn't wait to get shot of such a long term, unpredictable and probably expensive liability as Olympic legacy, complied with enthusiasm.

James Graven:

With the arrival of a new Mayor everything to do with the LDA was perceived by the incoming people as bloated, wasteful of resources, inefficient and even corrupt. There was a lot of fear in the LDA — fear of being unreasonably branded as inefficient, or simply fear of losing their jobs. Cost-cutting was the priority, and the way to do that was to take people out and stop programmes. There was a big review. The LDA lost its Chief Executive, Manny Lewis, and the GLA lost all the previous mayoral advisers, except for Neale Coleman, who was perceived by senior figures, including Sebastian Coe, to be essential for the Olympics. The LDA was ultimately run down, while legacy responsibilities were passed over to the newly formed OPLC.

Around mid 2008, there was a decision taken by central government and by government in London that we needed a distinct legacy body to take ownership and be the custodian of legacy. There was, I think, a recognition that legacy was at risk at this stage.

Neale Coleman:
We set up the legacy board of advisers. Why did we do it at this point? Well, we needed more attention on the legacy and something independent of the ODA that was going to continue after the Games. And to be fair, a lot of people were saying — well, what are we going to do there afterwards? Off the back of all that, we started discussions with Government about a legacy vehicle.

We decided we would establish a 50:50 Companies Act company, the OPLC (to be run by Hazel Blears at the Department for Communities and Local Government), Tessa Jowell at DCMS and Boris Johnson. It was the three of them running the show. A deal was done and it was a very agonising process indeed. But we did the deal and we did the land transfer. The land would come across to the OPLC. We then did the OPLC to the London Legacy Development Corporation (LLDC) deal, which meant we then had a real legacy vehicle owning the land.

James Graven:

The decision was taken that the DCLG, DCMS and London Government would have three-way ownership of legacy — 50% owned by central government, split between the two departments, and 50% by the Mayor. And they would set up a dedicated legacy body, which would become known as the OPLC. The OPLC would take all the LDA's legacy activity out of the LDA. The implication was that the LDA would retrench and focus on the rest of London. The OPLC was constituted in summer 2009. It took a long period of gestation to get the governance arrangements established and working.

Margaret Ford (former Chair of English Partnerships and therefore well known to the Government as a safe pair of hands) was appointed as Chair of the OPLC in May 2009, and then Andy Altman, the Chief Executive, arrived in August 2009. (Andy was less well known over here, an American planner who had made his name as Director of the well regarded Anacostia Waterfront Initiative, in Washington DC). I was effectively appointed by Neale to help Margaret set the company up and provide the interface and the coordination with the three owners, the three founding members as they were known.

The process was launched to get the board in place. A large, heavy-hitting board was created. The tripartite ownership arrangement carried on for a short period, but it was a difficult set-up, with the three bodies constantly debating things. Meanwhile, as governance arrangements were being created, the body of work on legacy had to continue. Officers worked under considerable personal strain because of the change to the LDA. Despite this, they managed to keep a lot of programmes intact. Now there would be a real body that would own the Park and its activities, rather than the ODA, a body that would be gone as soon as the Park was built.

Margaret Ford was seen as the absolute saviour when she came along. She was appointed by Boris Johnson even though she was a crossbench peer. She was the acceptable face for everyone, and when she joined, she made it her business to meet everyone, from the local boroughs through to private sector people. She brought in her connections with central government politicians as well, so she was seen as hugely credible, personable and well liked. She and Newham Mayor Robin Wales really hit it off, for example. They worked out that they grew up within eight miles of each other, in the same part of Scotland. She was charismatic and made people feel welcome. Suddenly, for the first time, there was a real person with whom people who had legacy interests could engage.

In August, Andy Altman joined from the United States as Chief Executive of OPLC. He arrived at a time when one of the big challenges was to make sure that the OPLC had land as well as people and money. Andy was very clear, on the basis of his American experiences, that to be an effective regeneration body with teeth, it had to have the land. That became a strong mantra that he and Margaret pushed over the ensuing year or so as they built the credibility of OPLC as the long-term credible owner of the story. Socio-economics came back on the agenda.

At that point, the land was owned by the LDA and had all this debt attached to it. It was transferred to the OPLC along with the debt. There's still an expectation that the development will all come good in the end, and that all the debt will be paid back.

The other organisational move that happened was the formation of an executive unit by the Olympic host boroughs and the development of their own strategy — the Strategic Regeneration Framework (SRF). This was branded as the convergence strategy: a vision that these boroughs would simply converge with the rest of London in terms of economic opportunities, health and life chances. The boroughs wrote their convergence strategy and Mayor Boris Johnson in turn wrote that vision into his London Plan. The SRF was significant politically because it privileged the boroughs once again. It said, 'we are not going over your heads to set the agenda for your area.'

The best slides I remember seeing were Andy Altman's. He showed the A-Z from 10 years ago from this area, the A-Z as it was in 2012, and the A-Z of what it would look like in the future. The 2003 A-Z showed white space for the Lower Lea. It looked like a tear in the fabric of London. Andy's slides showed how all the change would stitch that fabric back together.

Paul Brickell:

Andy Altman was appointed as the Olympic Park Legacy Company's Chief Executive, and Margaret Ford was Chair. They both connected locally in a very positive way. Andy knew that we needed to make it more than a physical regeneration programme, and he saw what Leaside was doing. That's why he brought me in. Andy drew this team together and asked me to lead it. Many organisations didn't really understand and saw the Games as a distraction, so we had to work very hard to mainstream the regeneration of the Park and legacy, which to a large extent we have done.

When I got to the OPLC in 2011, which then became the LLDC in 2012, we acted with this approach in mind. At that point, the Olympic Park was shut while the Games venues were being constructed. We told the story about the area outside the Park, engaging with how the Park could unfold. By the time it reopened, we had put the stitches in place. We did many things to re-engage with areas outside the Park — developing the White Building as a cultural centre at an approach road into the Park and reinstating boat tours. Our strategy wasn't to focus on gates opening, rather on acts of unfolding. That's what we tried to do. We sought to suggest that the Park could already be open in our heads and that we could make things happen that unfolded the opening now, working towards the day when it would be fully open. We were asking: where can we do this and where not? Where is it open? Where is it tight?

Richard Brown:
>Everything to do with the Olympic Park and local regeneration went into the Legacy Company. I think that's one of the lessons. You need to be clear with legacy: make sure exactly what it is, because it's such an overused word. And if you use it to try and cover everything, it becomes so broad it loses all meaning. It's a bit like the term 'sustainability'. It basically becomes 'all good things'. We had a clear, local focus.
>
>The Olympic Park Legacy Company was set up. Margaret Ford and Andy Altman were appointed. Margaret and Tom Russell had a very rapid parting of ways. The stadium contributed to it. Tom, making the best of a bad job, to be honest, had been fostering this idea of a living stadium, which would be an educational and community facility when not hosting athletics. Margaret took the view that that was going to be a disaster and that we needed to revisit the football option. Anyway, Tom vanished and Andy Altman appeared.
>
>One outstanding issue for OPLC was getting control of the Olympic Park land. The LDA owned the land, and the land had debt hanging over it from the purchase. The LDA didn't want to transfer the asset to the new legacy company without also transferring the risk and liability for the debt. But if they had transferred the asset and the liability to OPLC, the new organisation would have been instantly rendered insolvent. The liability was in the order of £1 billion, or something like that. And the asset book value was £138 million.
>
>Eventually the Government took the debt onto its books, so the LDA could then say goodbye to the land. They wouldn't

transfer the staff over until they transferred the land over because the staff function was attached to the land. It just took ages, until October 2010, for that transaction to be completed. So there was a slightly odd situation up until 2010, when everyone from the LDA was seconded to the legacy company.

Richard Brown:

In the run up to the 2010 General Election, Boris Johnson started to talk to the Government and to his colleagues in the Conservative Party about getting more powers for the Mayor of London.

I think they were receptive for all sorts of reasons. The one thing they discussed was whether to establish a new structure, a mayoral development corporation for the Olympic Park. They were talking about turning the OPLC into some new kind of development corporation. Did we want it? And if we did want it — given that part of the Government's proclaimed and not unreasonable objective was to rationalise a few agencies in the Lower Lea Valley — how wide did we want it to go? How to set it up? And should it have — and I was surprised this was on the table — planning policy powers as well as planning decisions powers?

The answer is obvious now in retrospect, though I personally still feel some ambivalence as to whether it is appropriate. It's a curious thing to give planning policy powers, the expression of a vision of a place, to an unelected body. The decision-making on its own is a matter of service delivery efficiency, but setting the policy framework is a question of democratic accountability. I think the feeling was that the boroughs weren't getting their act together, so some sort of Plan B was needed. And it fitted into the localism agenda.

I had some reservations about some aspects of the new LLDC, but one thing that I wholeheartedly think is good is the clear accountability to the Mayor of London. Working in a central government agency, the possibilities of sinning or going astray are limited because every aspect of your life is controlled. It's impossible to conceive of a heretical thought. By contrast, the accountability model in the GLA is, 'do your job, be intelligent about when you talk to us and when you talk to the Mayor, and manage your relationships properly. And by the way, if you screw up, you're out.' You're given free will, but you may end up making the wrong decision. It was a good model for the LLDC.

Neale Coleman:
Margaret Ford, Chair of the OPLC, tried very hard and came very close to pulling off a deal for the BBC to move into the International Broadcasting Centre once it was available, with Eastenders and Strictly Come Dancing. It was a real blow when that deal wasn't secured before the Games.

It was the last building that LOCOG was going to hand over after the Games because there was a lot of stuff to strip out. They were due to hand it over to us at the end of January 2013, and in the middle of January 2013, we got a call from BT, who said, 'we want to put BT Sport in there; we need to have our studio completely fitted out and ready to broadcast by the end of May or we're going to go to Salford.' This was in the middle of January. There was no lease and no planning. We took a lot of risks. Most of the credit rests with BT, who did an incredible job in terms of fitting out. Jamie Young, who ran the Games for the BBC, says it would have taken the BBC six years. BT did it in four months. Remarkable really. But Dennis Hone, Chief Executive of LLDC took a lot of risks, rightly.

Once we had BT in there, that really underpinned the deal. Now we had this huge data centre moving in, we had Loughborough coming in, and we were going to get UCL and the Institute of Robotics in there, and the Advanced

Propulsion Centre. We had loads of high-tech research and development, media, technology, you name it, in the middle of nowhere! It was just phenomenal. We were spending £18 million doing up Hackney Wick Station. But it was exactly what Hackney wanted. It's a miracle! But it's terrific.

Here East (the innovation and technology campus developed in the former Olympic Media Centre) is a triumph for everyone. Dennis Hone did a good job. We had to publicly finance the International Broadcasting Centre and the Main Press Centre originally expected to be provided by the private sector, and there was a long fight to make sure that the building was permanent. But nobody really knew what would happen to it, particularly the International Broadcasting Centre, which has 11 metre floor-to-ceiling heights.

Ralph Ward:

The original legacy plan had been to fill much of the former Games space with high density housing, most of which was actually going to be out of reach of most local residents. This was a strange echo of the situation in 1995 when Minister David Curry, to the frustration of Conor McAuley had announced that the Lea Valley was the place to put lots and lots of housing rather than as a place to foster economic growth.

Boris Johnson's stint as Mayor did spark one very significant — and positive — shift in legacy development planning. Not the weird Arcelor Mittal Tower, whose sole purpose seems to be to house a slide which foreign students on visits to the Park seem inexplicably drawn to launching themselves down, but the plan to build a cluster of important national and metropolitan cultural institutions on the Park. Originally (but no longer) known as Olympicopolis, the arrival of institutions of this stature east of the River Lea is a new departure for London and game-changing for the area. Which is actually what the Olympics was all about.

Neale Coleman:

Boris Johnson, London's second Mayor, wasn't happy with the legacy communities scheme. He thought it was under-exciting. The boroughs felt the same way. So he pushed, 'can't we do a bit more here?'

At the same time, discussions were going on between UCL and Newham about developing Carpenters (housing estate). It became clear that Carpenters could not happen. But we did succeed in agreeing that UCL was potentially interested in coming to the park. That expression of interest was the first brick in the wall. This has all been so opportunistic!

We decided we would assemble a group of culture people to come and talk about what we could do culturally in the Olympic Park. Martin Rothman of the V&A came to the meeting and said some interesting things in it. As we were going out, I grabbed Martin, and Mayor Boris came over. We got in a huddle in the corner and Martin said, 'well, you know, we might be, yeah ... this is interesting.'

A fortnight after that, Dennis Hone saw in a newspaper that Sadlers Wells wanted a site for a new theatre. He rang up Alistair Spalding out of the blue and said, 'you know, you could come here.' I can't remember how we got on to University of the Arts London. I think it became clear when we were talking that they were interested. And then we start looking for something foreign, and we start talking to everybody, from the Guggenheim in Bilbao to Getty. And then Boris got an invite to go and speak at a session at the Smithsonian. When you think about it, it's been quite opportunistic, but why not? How else would you do it?

Ralph Ward:

Olympic rhetoric talked rather loosely about the 'transformation of the Lower Lea Valley,' but in practice the Olympic Park occupies only a small part of it. With the vast majority of the massive Olympic budget focused only on this limited area, and ignoring the rest, awkward questions were left about whether the remainder of the Valley would benefit at all. In the words of Tim Williams, former CEO of the Thames Gateway Partnership, it might simply 'show up' the poverty of the surrounding area rather than 'show off' its potential.

How to mitigate this risk was a matter of concern to a wide range of planners, urban designers and landscape architects involved. Below, Richard Rutter talks about the long standing enhancement programmes which he managed for British Waterways over a number of years to improve the river valley. Jason Prior, landscape lead on Park design, talks about his concern to maximise the impact of the Park on the surrounding area and the value of extending the boundaries of the Olympic zone. Eleanor Fawcett, the urban designer working on the Lea Valley for the GLA, outlines the role and aims of the Olympic Area Planning Framework, and the 'Olympic fringe' programmes, in which she played a central part.

Richard Rutter:
> I had been involved in the Lower Lea since 1984, when I was a student working for the Lea Valley Regional Park and I worked there from 1986 to 2002. Then I joined British Waterways in 2002. The reason I moved was to restore and regenerate the Lower Lea and Bow Back Rivers on behalf of British Waterways. We organised boat tours in the 1980s, looking at all the factories. Some of them were still standing at that time of course, but the Lower Lea Valley was desolate and derelict into the late 1980s.
>
> In the late 1960s and early 1970s, a lot of the emphasis with Lea Valley Regional Park (LVRP) was on leisure facilities like sports centres, running tracks and swimming pools. When I joined, the focus had started to change towards open space, countryside areas and access to green space. At an early stage, my job was to develop that country park ethos, and restore and improve areas between the built facilities. By the late 1980s and early 1990s, London boroughs began to extend their leisure facilities, taking advantage of Sports Lottery Funding. This meant competition with the Lea Valley Regional Park Authority for facilities like squash courts and swimming pools. The LVRP emphasis on the open space grew in importance, so we focused on the intrinsic qualities of green space and the heritage of the Lea Valley.
>
> In the Lower Lea, improving the countryside area led us to focus on the Bow Ecology Park at Three Mills, the Leamouth Peninsula, and the East India Dock Basin at the mouth of the Lea. Upstream, the focus included the marshlands at Walthamstow, Hackney and Tottenham Marshes, and higher up to the old gravel workings around Cheshunt and Broxbourne. There were Sites of Special Scientific Interest in the Lea Valley, including Walthamstow Marshes and the reservoirs, which are important for migratory birds. Later, with funds from the Government's SRB, we were able to restore

some of the industrial heritage, repair and restore the green ecology, and make connections between green spaces and urban areas.

There is a story of the countryside and open space that sits with the story of heritage and history, stitching them together, and people did get excited about it. There were 30 medicinal herbs on Walthamstow Marshes, for instance. What could we do to get people interested? We employed a medical herbalist to host a walk and talk about these medicinal herbs. We had about 150 people turn up on a Sunday morning wanting to learn about them. Wow! We didn't know this was such an area of interest. When the Olympics came along, all the work on green space enhancement accelerated.

When I think back to the early days, I remember Deputy Prime Minister John Prescott coming to visit the area before the Government had fully committed to the Olympic bid. We took him out on a Rigid Inflatable Boat, which can move quite fast. One of the guys on the bank said, 'shout if you want to go faster John.' And he said, 'bugger off!' And he got it. Prescott got it. We were having a real laugh, and we were on the Limehouse Cut and one of these East End lads, about 16 or 17, said, 'hey that's Tony Prescott!' He said, 'I get that all the bloody time!'

Since 2005, over £60m has been invested into the waterways, on projects including tow paths, dredging, Three Mills Lock, waterway walls and pontoons. We would never have had investment without the Olympics. But the boundaries of the Olympics meant that Three Mills was left out. Three Mills could have been a real hub of activity for the Olympics, an educational and heritage resource.

The first master plan advocated cutting back the waterway walls and creating a huge natural riverside, almost like a tidal floodplain and estuary with birds and what have you. British Waterways knew it might have been feasible, but it wasn't viable. You would have lost a lot of land which was needed for the Olympic Sports venues. If you had cut the banks, you would also have found contamination behind the walls. The big concrete walls which were built in the 1930s were a significant flood defence system.

The Environment Agency said, 'over our dead bodies are you going to build a lock to impound the waterways!' However, we are still alive and we've done it. It was really painful at the time. We thought 'What are you doing?' One, you haven't got the space to do what you want to do and, two, trying to naturalise the valley is just not viable. It's feasible but it's not viable, because the cost of breaking out those walls and moving those banks back was a non-starter. Yet it took 18 months, maybe even more, to come back to a more realistic vision for the Olympic Park.

The big move was the impoundment of the waterway. Previously, there was very little water in the main Waterworks River next to the Aquatic Centre. Because the area was tidal, twice a day it would have gone down to the level of a concrete channel with smelly mud, trolleys and God only knows what. Also, you need to bear in mind that tidal flows meant that at times you wouldn't have enough water to sail in, and then at high tide it would be too high to go under the bridges. The whole idea was to make the water more accessible to the flow of both people and water transport. To achieve those objectives we had to control the water level. We created a tidally controlled system at Three Mills with a tidal lock adjacent to fish-belly gates which allows fish to pass through. British Waterways made it possible for people to enjoy the water spaces in and around the Olympic Park.

Michael Owens:
This sense of the wider area was an issue for Jason Prior, design lead with EDAW on the master-planning and urban

design of the Olympic Park and the Lower Lea in support of the Olympic bid, and the early stages of implementation. He regrets that the Park didn't extend to a much bigger and more varied area.

Jason Prior:

I always thought we could put our hands around more of the surrounding area. I'm talking specifically about the thing we know as the Olympic Park. I wanted the Park gates back in Hackney Wick or on the other side of the A12. I wanted more people to be living in the Park, not by increasing the amount of green space, but by pushing out the management regime and the entry, so when you came through the Park gates, you might still be another half a mile from the green space, in a sort of 'Park land'.

Our early thoughts about integration were that you didn't have to build new to integrate, you just had to redefine the geographic boundaries. I think Hackney Wick and Carpenters Lane are psychologically seen now as being outside the Olympic Park. They are a different place. Whereas if we'd changed the way we talked, I think we — and the organisation responsible for it — would have taken a different philosophical approach.

I remember we did that piece of work on how many canal bridges were needed on the western boundary. I remember walking around bits of London — up in St John's Wood and around the canals running through the East End. I remember taking a weekend out, going to Amsterdam with my Brompton (bicycle), and just cycling around canals. It rained all weekend. I was literally pacing out how things worked. I remember going out to the new developments in the harbour where they'd got it right. I was thinking, 'What granularity do you need?' And I remember we did all those diagrams with bridges, and we did all that work on land acquisition to connect things.

And then the bridges got chopped, either for cost reasons or because of 'complications'. They became a job for 'legacy', and you just knew the moment had passed. I always thought bigger, not in terms of building more, but in terms of stewardship. I thought the local authorities missed the boat at this point. We'd had this discussion about the bigger zone, we spent all that time with the Mayor's team about connections, and then literally overnight the boundaries came in. Maybe the Government couldn't wrap their head around the idea that there'd be one thing that you would build, but there might be a bigger thing that you might want to own the direction of. You didn't need to spend money all over it, but you had to have control. We could never get people to understand that the inner core and the fence line didn't have to be the same as the 'administrative' boundary — that those two things could be different.

I think that if they had understood it, two things would have happened at a socio-economic level. You would have immediately pulled more people in. Which, yes, created a 'problem' because you had a bigger constituency to deal with. But at heart I'm the sort of person who feels you should engage with communities. In this field that's what it's all about. I think you could have gone wider, to a constituency that valued everything that was going on. You'd have immediately put the local authorities in a stronger position. These may all be good reasons why people didn't want to do it!

The smaller the area, the more it reduces the ability of the Olympic Park to swing the pendulum in the East End of London in a positive direction. Take Stratford High Street. Some unmitigated crap has gone up along there. We did all that work on carefully balanced housing provision, looking for a balanced community in this relatively small area of London, and then we ringed it with a forest of one-bedroom micro-flats. I remember early on, we were looking for things like stability. We were looking for people to take an interest in schools and to invest in the community, as opposed to trying to make enough money to get out of the area. And it seemed to me that the bigger the piece of the map you could pull into that sense of ownership of the big idea, the more chance you had of that really working.

Michael Owens:

For those of us who had been engaged in the regeneration of the Lea Valley over the years preceding the idea of the Olympics, Jason's proposition that the masterplan should focus on a wider geography was music. We were also interested in how the masterplanners would address the design of the Park itself.

Jason Prior:

I'd look at it at two levels I suppose — the macro park scale, the river interventions, the wetlands, all of that. The North Park I think is substantially as I would have hoped. I think structurally the South Park is good. I've heard people criticise that we've still got things like vertical canal walls and river walls, but you have no idea what was stuck behind. That is a legacy of a much deeper history of the site.

The South Park is filling up with a lot of stuff, and I think if you look at these exhibition-type amusement parks in London — the Vauxhall Pleasure Gardens and Crystal Palace — they tend to go through a cycle. You try things out, and if it works it stays, and if it doesn't, or the fashion changes, it comes down. I could see the South Park changing probably every 10 or 15 years. I think that's fine because it's about satisfying a real need in the here and now, in an urban park setting that will ultimately respond to the nature of the population that grows up around it, if the dialogue between Park management and community is strong enough.

My assumption is that the North Park will change less. It's more in keeping with how I saw the overall Park, which was simpler than how it was either built for the Games or transitioned in legacy.

I come from a more English landscape romantic parkland background. As a landscape architect, I am interested in landscape structure and the larger story of landscape green infrastructure in the service of a bigger city system. The restoration of the ecology of the Lea, the creation of the flood plain in the sunken valley, all that was what I felt passionate about. I am extremely proud that we got all of that in, that big ecological content, the way that the rivers work. To me that is the heart of that Park.

Do you remember the big push to build up to the river? The densifying visions? I was deeply troubled by those heavy pushes to scale down the green park and create more development space. We went down the line of this bigger, more naturalistic feature, a sort of deeper urbanisation in the context of the wider Lea Valley. I always talked about the transect from the Thames to the rural hinterland of London, and I loved the idea of a park that de-industrialised as it went north. It was an easy idea to explain to people.

I always felt that the better urban outcomes were something you could deliver further south down the Lea Valley, south of the railway line. I don't think people understood that there were some very significant areas of land down there — the gas holders, for example, and the area around the lock, that could be essential parts of the legacy scheme.

A problem with 'grand projects' is that all the tendency is to put all the desirable elements into the one place where you've got control. What we were trying to say in the opportunity framework (the planning strategy for the wider Lea Valley, which EDAW also led on, working under the direction of the GLA) was that you could locate some of the critical legacy elements further down in the Lower Lea Valley below the Olympic Park. Such legacy projects would still be somewhere within the halo of the Olympic Park project. Not only were you placing these catalytic buildings and uses nearer to more deprived communities who needed them, but you also could use their presence as a trigger for higher quality outcomes in those areas where all we've got now is opportunistic land development. This would also have allowed more of the big open qualities of the Olympic Park to be retained.

We had been trying to create a sort of romantic ideal of English parkland, a flowing romantic landscape, where the sports buildings were like pavilions. Remember that big discussion about why we wanted the velodrome visible at the top of the Park, and the stadium anchoring the bottom, and other buildings that just touch on the Park edge? It was a classical landscape structure.

The other thing was the standard we set about the usability of the Park from a disability and access point of view, the way that we managed to lay out all those contours so that everywhere worked — there was nowhere that you couldn't access.

Eleanor Fawcett:

We were trying to bring together the physical changes in the area so the place would end up functioning as a bit of London, not as a collection of places on the edge of the Park that become problematic. We set out to encourage thinking and planning for physical changes that could dovetail with social and economic changes.

The strategy in the OAPF firstly aimed to create three new town centres to support population growth: West Ham, Bromley by Bow and Hackney Wick. Secondly, our intention was to create a linear green spine. Thirdly, we sought to rationalise the industry in ways that would enable what was left to survive and grow. And fourthly, we aimed to create links between the core and the fringe neighbourhoods. All these ideas were set out in the OAPF. I've never heard anyone else present it like that. Others suggest that there is the Olympic Park and then other stuff around it, which I don't think is the story at all.

I worked very closely with Sarah Elliott, the planner in the GLA who led the work on the OAPF. Allies and Morrison and EDAW were commissioned to produce the plans. That period gave me an in-depth sense of the Lower Lea Valley as a whole place, compared with the perspective of most people who just nibble at bits of it and never really appreciate the interplay.

The proposed town centres are important. We envisaged town centres at the populated edges of the valley, as places that would functionally straddle the divide between the Park and what lay beyond. We made life hard for ourselves by creating new town centres in the hardest possible places, on the dividing line. It would have been easier to create some brand new town centres down the middle in their own world: a very introverted strategy. Existing places would have limped along, downtrodden and ignored.

We were desperately trying to take the nuggets of what already existed and grow them into places you would think of as successful. We imagined democratic, civic spaces, where people would feel welcome whether they were spending money or hanging out. Those might be public external spaces, they could be like the White Building at Hackney Wick, or a community centre or playground. We used the label 'places of exchange.' Another one-liner we used in the OAPF was the 'tear in the fabric' — the idea that all the connective tissue in this place had been torn apart and that new stitches were needed to reconnect the Lower Lea into the urban fabric.

When the Opportunity Area Planning Framework was finished, I proposed that we produce several Olympic fringe master plans to set the priorities. It was a logical next step from the OAPF. They included Hackney Wick/Fish Island, Bromley by Bow and Sugar House Lane, Stratford High Street, Leyton, or what became known as the northern Olympic fringe in Stratford, and a landscape strategy for Hackney Marshes and the southern Olympic fringe neighbourhoods including Poplar and Canning Town.

In 2008, new Mayor Boris Johnson appointed Peter Bishop to run Design for London, GLA's urban design team. Design for London managed to secure a capital budget and suddenly we were able to fund several projects identified within the Olympic fringe masterplans, including £12m to spend on Olympic fringe projects. We delivered the White Building, Hackney Marshes changing facilities, public realm improvements in Leyton and Three Mills Green, and we contributed to works in Stratford. We were able to build stuff and show what we meant. We worked in partnership with the LTGDC and the boroughs on several projects. By 2010, the Olympic Host Boroughs Organisation had been established, and these projects became subsumed into their £100m public realm programme

I developed 10 strategic packages, with the focus on key routes leading into the Olympic Park and key town centres. I then took on a role in signing off projects before they could proceed. This all took place in the run-up to the Games in 2010/2011, and the projects were finished before the Games in summer 2012. So 2011 was the big time. And then they happened, and nobody noticed, because the one thing that I never managed to do was to get anyone to do any publicity around it. It's like an invisible project.

Because we had less than three years to deliver the public realm programme in the run-up to the Games, we didn't address the trickiest projects. After the Games, I joined the

London Legacy Development Corporation, and there I tried to push those schemes that were in the 'too difficult box', because otherwise they would never happen. That's why Stratford Station, Hackney Wick Station and Bromley by Bow Station are all getting LLDC money spent on them, and they are all happening. The A12 study has resulted in new crossings. It's the role of the LLDC to do that heavy lifting because nobody else can, or is prepared to. It's the same with the ambition to complete the Lea Valley Regional Park by making the connection down to the River Thames.

I think that we've done really well on local connectivity and pedestrian and cycle connectivity. In my view, our success is a result of pushing to be very precise in the Opportunity Area Planning Framework. We resisted generalities like 'area of search for a new bridge', and insisted on 'one here, one here, one here'. We have been able to get developers to deliver quite a lot of those links, particularly in and around the Olympic Park, but also further south like Sugar House Lane, where they are delivering a new bus bridge over to Bromley by Bow. It remains tough to address the need for connections across the heavy infrastructure like the A12 and the railway lines. We focused hard on the idea of mixing uses. For example, we developed policies around 'industry plus mix'. The policy allowed new developments in former industrial areas that could include housing but should not result in a loss of industrial or commercial floor space. We set a challenge to developers and landowners to be creative, perhaps stack the work space or have it on the ground floor. We encouraged them to be creative in intensifying the use of land.

Sugar House Lane and Hackney Wick are the two places where that policy has played itself out so far. You always end up thinking, 'Oh it's not as good as it could've been', but both, I think, really show that you can bring interesting partners to the table and get a much richer conversation going when you impose slightly complicated policies like that. I think they are going to be better places for it. You always end up having to do deals, but the starting point is so clear that people say, 'Oh okay, I can get my head around that and I can see that there are interesting ways of doing it.' Some developers are starting to connect with eloquent, interesting local businesses like Dalston Cola and the artists, saying sophisticated things about the way the area is changing.

We funded the White Building on the banks of the canal at Hackney Wick, right at the edge of the Park. We completed the project two years before the Games, delivering a mixed use creative centre including studios, a residency space and a bar/restaurant/event space.

You can take people to the White Building on the banks of the canal at Hackney Wick and they'll say, 'oh wow, this is really cool.' And they will understand what you're saying about Hackney Wick, y'know, to people who aren't from that world and find it a bit intimidating. I think it's quite successful in breaking down barriers between the creative community and developers and investors. Next to it is a skate park, so it's not all about artists, it's about getting the local kids in as well. And now we've got the funding to redevelop Hackney Wick station and the land owned by the LLDC around the station, so there's an interesting story unfolding about different ways the public sector can help grow an area over time.

We set out a strategy in the OAPF, and I'm really pleased that over 10 years it did culminate in some built projects! There's so much criticism of strategies just becoming dusty on the shelf and never having any impact, so it was nice to do projects that created a benchmark. When you were talking to developers you could say, 'This is the quality that we require.' Or your projects could demonstrate that there was a market. For example, we had always wanted family housing on Sugar House Lane, and by creating a park at Three Mills Green, an amazing park with a playground and people, we signalled that this was a place for families. The White Building in Hackney Wick enabled us to say to developers, 'Look, there are thousands of artists in this area, and you can develop schemes that create space for them.' Each of the projects provide lessons to be learned. Not all of them are amazing; often they were experimental. I'm just so happy that we got to deliver them using the momentum of the Games, because otherwise they probably wouldn't have happened.

When we did the White Building, there were some who said, 'why there? It isn't even in the Olympic Park?' Some key officers were different, like Andrew Gaskell, who took us under his wing and basically steamrollered it through. He really protected us and enabled it to happen. He did the same for other projects and it was tragic that he died.

Hopefully Hackney Wick is still going to be a fantastic scheme. We managed to get all the other landowners on board, but commitment to a town centre that is much more than housing, and which captures the creative qualities of the local community, feels so fragile and vulnerable. It needs people who stay committed to the big picture, who understand that the developments on the Park — here in the east, at the media centre, the neighbourhoods of Eastwick and Sweetwater — they all need a good town centre at Hackney Wick to succeed.

If you get someone excited about what you're trying to achieve, and you take them on the journey with you, planners or developers, then you've got some chance of getting there, because you're both trying to achieve the same thing. You have to find the people you can excite about the outcome, and then you've got a chance. I hope that's where I can come in, helping unlock things and make them happen. Because I've been doing it for so long, I've somehow ended up being one of the old timers of the Lower Lea Valley, which is a bit ironic.

Anon:

It's interesting that the Westfield scheme includes champagne bars. I just wondered who was going to sit and drink champagne, but despite some people's prejudices it turns out there are obviously people from Newham who drink champagne.

Richard Brown:

We learned several lessons from the Olympics. You know I've thought about this quite a bit. A lot of it sounds like the bleeding obvious, but the extent to which they're not doing it in Rio de Janeiro demonstrates that these factors need to be emphasised.

Get everyone tied in and agreed on how it's going to operate. The Olympics will always involve partnerships between different tiers in government, and having a problem-solving and coordination mechanism, which in London was the Olympic Board, is important. (The Board brought together both the Secretary of State, and the London Mayor, to ensure collaborative working between national and local politicians). Apart from a bit of a spat between the BOA and LOCOG about sponsorship, there have been no rows that have broken cover, despite changes of administration at national and regional government levels at different times. I think that's quite impressive. There have been plenty of disagreements, but they've been resolved privately.

Put the organising committee — as the producers of the show — and the builders of the stage in the same building. This seems trivial, but it was important to the success of the London scheme. Put them together from the outset. It won't make the relationship completely plain sailing because it never can be, but they should then be able to 'pop into each other's offices to have a row' rather than have the 'sending angry emails to each other' kind of row.

It's never too early to start planning for legacy. And that was the one to-be-determined area that we hadn't resolved in 2004 when we made the bid. There were issues like the size of the stadium. The sand was going through the hourglass, and they had to decide to build this 80,000-seater stadium going down to 25,000 seats so that the stadium would deliver an athletics legacy. Most people think that 25,000 seats were neither one thing nor the other. It's big and expensive, but not big enough to host football and potentially have a viable use. But they ran out of time to get football in there and they didn't have a clear legacy owner in place. And I think the government was unwilling to take the risk at that time of being left with an 80,000-seater white elephant. Ultimately, for all the focus on legacy, when you've got time ticking away and your job is to build for the Games as the ODA, then your job is to build for the Games. I think that's one thing that we didn't quite get right.

The training and skills programmes took longer than they should have to get going. The organisational responsibilities for delivering those aspects of the scheme took some time to resolve.

How one thinks of the Olympics as part of the city plan is a conceptual issue. Mayor Ken Livingstone envisaged the ways in which the Olympics would be aligned with his vision and plan. 'I will only support a bid for the 2012 Olympics if it is in East London.' There were people who said, 'why don't you centre it on Wembley?'. And he said, 'I'm not going to support it if it's centred on Wembley. I'm not interested.' The Olympics brings a huge focus of investment and public attention, so he wanted to use that to further his strategic aims of securing investment in a deprived part of the city.

Don't try to retrofit a strategy to a bid. If you don't know why you're doing it, where you're doing it — apart from the fact you want to have the Olympics — then you need to think long and hard, because the danger is that you're going to waste it.

Kevin Whittle:

The LTGDC ran from 2007 to 2012. It never had a huge amount of money or a huge amount of land. It was a half-hearted attempt at something that might have worked quite well if the forward strategy had been for the development corporation's boundary to expand to encompass the whole of the Olympic Park, the whole of the Lower Lea Valley. And then for the legacy Park and all those sites to be delivered by a Canary Wharf type structure with a development corporation pulling it all together for the public rather than the client.

There's no evidence of the Lower Lea Valley really being linked to the Olympic Park. There's still no evidence of it, and that's bad. It will happen one day. I don't think politicians ever really get to grips because they don't think long enough ahead, do they? In every meeting at that time, I used to say, 'Canary Wharf was 12 years old when they got to their 10 million square feet out of their 20. That's how long it takes. Look at Southbank. Southbank took 25, 30 years and it is still a work in progress.'

Michael Keith:

Whether the Olympics was a benefit or a curse, I think will be a judgement of history in the longer term. I think it probably is a benefit in the Borough, but not nearly as much as the hubris would suggest.

Do I see a shape to what's happening in the Lower Lea now? That's funny. You see, I think the test will be the Wick. I think that's why I find the Wick quite an interesting space now, because there does seem to be a sense of quite a lot being up for grabs. I think King's Cross is an interesting space. I think the property developers for that scheme, Argent, have done quite a good job in King's Cross. It's quite interesting, being partly for educational use, partly for other kinds of post-industrial city use, as well as for other kinds of employment use. When you say it's worked, it's certainly worked a lot better than a lot of other places, and I suppose one of the tests of what's happening in the Lea is whether you get development in a way that's more sympathetic than just 27 blocks of flats. When you go down Bow Road and off into Stratford, you just see tower after tower, architectural shit ...

Sandra Hunt:

Before the Olympics, the inspirational person was Heseltine. Heseltine was about the only person in Government I've ever known who had a real vision, and the drive and the foresight to see the potential of the area. Big-scale interventions in the 1980s like Canary Wharf may have had their issues but they delivered results, even if they were often viewed in a bad light. Much later, the New Labour model was a different way of thinking about regeneration, focused on the socio-economic rather than the physical. There was some acceptance that physical investment was important, but when the Olympics came along, suddenly there was a drive, a means and a mechanism.

The Olympics unlocked money, for undergrounding the power lines, for example, and that was useful, but it wasn't really part of the concept of the Arc. We hadn't envisioned a stadium and sports facilities. I assumed there'd be far more leisure in a different sort of way — not exclusive leisure but sports facilities. The stadium is an insulated environment. The Aquatic Centre is good, though it is just a bit too dominant, in that it was a set piece that landed on East London; it wasn't necessarily tailored for what was needed then. It brought money, but not necessarily for what was needed. But it did bring money, and beggars can't be choosers. It wasn't what I would have personally chosen. If we'd had that money without the Olympics that would have been fantastic.

At one level, I think the Olympics was fantastically successful. It exceeded everyone's expectations and I think Londoners really got behind it in a way I hadn't envisaged. And it was a community event in many ways. I don't think you can overestimate how successful it was. That's all good and there is also a place for a legacy, but is it one of London's great places? I don't know. We'll have to see how London judges it. I'm not in a position to judge. Now it does feel very much like it's a place of its own. It doesn't feel particularly integrated with the whole of Stratford or even Hackney yet. I don't know whether that will work. It's hard to tell how it will work.

Conor McAuley:
Westfield was spectacularly right about the punt they took. They've still got consent within their planning permission to develop many more houses than those already constructed. When people look at the numbers lined up for the Olympic Park, they always overlook Westfield's consent. I'm horrified by the density levels. They're like Hong Kong densities. But I'm not going to get annoyed about it, so there you go. But what they're doing is reducing the level of affordable housing — a lot less affordable housing than they were supposed to have; they were meant to over-provide.

Having spent some years on the board of the London Docklands Development Corporation, I grew to like what development corporations could do. The problem we had with Stratford was that we drew the wrong planning boundaries consistently. We should have included both sides of Stratford High Street within the scheme. We had a boundary down the middle of the High Street. Stratford High Street is a mess because neither agency, the Olympic Development Authority nor the LTGDC took it seriously because it was on each of their boundaries. The ODA at that point wasn't interested in the outside of the Park. Their key priority quite obviously was getting the Park right. Nobody would look at Stratford High Street. It's a dog's dinner. And that's partly our fault. When the London Legacy Development Company boundaries were being looked at, I pushed for the whole piece to be considered, but there was resistance to it.

Paul Brickell:

Up at Here East, postgraduate students are starting their courses at the International Broadcast Centre and we're delivering an outreach course to local unemployed graduates. We've got 20 or so to sign up. The fairground with the beach that we have here now is a commercial operation, but for the next couple of weeks, many primary school kids will get on the rides for free. We've been able to combine the commercial and the community dimensions.

At the same time, they're getting ready to open the Institute of Robotics. Hackney Wick was a Wi-Fi cold spot for a long time and is now massively connected. The first 5,000 office space jobs are here in the International Quarter. Westfield's buzzing and full of local kids working for a living. And then we've got these big institutions: UCL, V&A, The Smithsonian and Sadlers Wells all coming in.

Someone said to me, 'oh you couldn't have dreamt of it.' I started to agree, but then I said, 'no actually we did. This is exactly what we dreamt of.' We dreamt that institutions of international renown and quality would want to come here because they saw opportunities for their own development. Because this is an exciting place. The people who live around here are exciting, and the institutions that they're meeting here are exciting. You get East London Dance, and Sadlers Wells, and local schools all here together and collaborating. It's amazing, and you think, 'yeah, that's what we wanted!' It feels like a big slice of what we dreamt of. The Park feels like it is becoming the astonishing place we wanted it to be.

There are a limited number of agencies and individuals who are the long-term custodians of an area. We have experienced projects that we have been involved with for over 25 years, like the redevelopment of St Andrews Hospital and the related reconfiguring of health provision in the area. Those of us who are rooted in the area feel that at times we are at the centre of setting policy and making things happen; at other times it feels like your ability to influence the agenda is drifting away.

Our role as a local community organisation like Bromley by Bow Centre, or the local authorities which have a longevity of 25 or 30 years or longer, is to be the long-term custodians. Sometimes, when control over the strategy for the area seems to be moving away as big players move in, it's worth the established local organisations setting a strategy, because at some point the responsibility for the strategy will all come back. That gives you the ability to let control slip away from you because you have the confidence that it will come back. In the meantime, you can do the things you can do while you're not at the centre of the story.

Eric Reynolds, Chief Executive of Trinity Buoy Wharf, consistently said that the realisation of the vision for the

Lower Lea was a 30-year project and the Olympics was going to be for six or eight of them. Lots of agencies come and go — the London Docklands Development Corporation, the London Development Agency, the London Thames Gateway Development Corporation, the London Committee for the Olympic Games, the ODA. The same is true in the health sector, with the primary care partnerships, primary care trusts, the inner Northeast London cluster, the outer Northeast London cluster, the CCGs, the East London Authority and then NHS London. How can any of those possibly be the custodians of a long-term vision when they're not around for long enough? You need bigger agencies to make bigger things happen, but you need the confidence to know that the long-term strategy will remain the responsibility of those rooted in local communities.

Richard Sumray:

I wrote a paper for George Osborne, whom I bumped into in the middle of the Games, outside the gymnastics in the Olympic family lounge. He was sitting there with his family and I went and sat down next to him by chance. I immediately had a go at him about the importance of achieving a strong legacy, and after about 10 minutes listening to me spouting at him, he said, 'well write me a paper.'

I wrote it as soon as the Games were finished and sent it to him, and it went into his red box. I haven't the faintest idea what happened to it after that, but I wrote about the importance of continuous Government involvement. One particular mistake was made. The Mayor, Boris Johnson, decided that after 2012 he would take responsibility for the regeneration of East London and take it away from Government. I believe that the Government should have continued to be integrally involved with ensuring the legacy was successful, as they had the necessary resources.

If you remember, back in 2002 or 2003, if you'd asked most of the public in London, 'could we host an Olympic Games?' the vast majority would have said, 'no way could we do that.' In their eyes, we just weren't capable of doing it. Our transport was awful and we could never build the facilities in time. Well look, the ODA and LOCOG did extraordinarily well. They built it all in time. They even completed some venues early, and as you know it was a hugely complex project. It is not my skill set but I thought they did terrifically well. I think the Games themselves were stunning. On the first Saturday, I was wandering around the Park. It was absolutely beautiful because of the meadows that had been planted.

I think we've got the best legacy of any Games and I have studied previous Games in depth. It is very good, but I still think the legacy set-up was wrong. I would have given legacy responsibility to the ODA, because I think it would have been stronger. There were two areas that could have been much better: sports participation and volunteering. Sport England did not think we could win the bid and did not put in the necessary effort before 2005 into how we could increase participation over the many years it would take to implement proposals. On volunteering, I was responsible for producing the first strategy for LOCOG and it focused on the legacy. In the end, though, LOCOG concentrated on the Games themselves and further proposals I made in 2011 were not accepted.

In the end, we did it. Thousands of people were involved in it, and performed fantastically well. The only thing I found difficult is when people claimed they were strongly supportive of the Games during the bid phase when I know many of them were strongly opposed at that time. I suppose people do that all the time. It's annoying, but one has to live with it. There were a lot of hangers-on who were desperately trying to get in on the act, and some managed to do so, but that's life, isn't it? That's the way it happens. The Games are always full of egos. I often felt I was a lone voice but by 2012 the whole country was behind it. The Games were highly successful and, on the whole, so is the legacy for East London.

Neale Coleman:

How important was the success of the Games to the realisation of legacy? 100% important. Crucial. Critical. Look at all the people who go to the Olympic Park today. Why would they go there if it weren't for the Olympics? When the Park reopened everyone was there; they were wearing all those Games Maker tops and Team GB tops. All the people who visited the Park — it was because of the Olympics. I always say this when I'm asked. The one thing you've got to do if you want a good legacy is to put on a terrific Games. If you don't do that, forget it.

We get criticisms: 'ohh you're not doing much housing' and 'you're not doing as much affordable housing'. And we say, 'but look, if we do all this in Stratford, and we create more jobs there, and we make an international destination there, and we create this fantastic metropolitan centre, it will lead to greater housing production in the surrounding area. It will drive investment in housing.' And I think that is probably right. To get significant employment at Stratford is no mean feat anyway, because you've already got the other employment centres. There's no reason for the jobs to leap out of Canary Wharf and go to Stratford really.

We had to work hard to get TfL. It was hard, hard work and to get the Financial Conduct Authority to move out to Stratford, I had to sweat blood. We nearly got Deutsche Bank. They were seriously talking about Stratford. In the end we didn't get it. They've gone to Canary Wharf. I think it will take a long time to get serious people to see Stratford as a viable alternative. It's in the right place and it's got the right transport, and all the rest of it, but it doesn't follow logically that it would have all those jobs there. With every single deal, you've got to spade and spade. You're banging your head against a wall for a long time. It's not a given!

The people who annoyed me most were the people who said, 'Stratford City would have happened anyway.' You had a global financial crisis going on! You're telling me it would have happened anyway, without the Olympics?! Do me a favour! It wouldn't have happened when it did. It might not have happened at all, and I can't understand anyone who doesn't get that.

What some said, wrongly, at that time, was, 'what have the Olympics ever done for us?' Have they ever been to the Lower Lea Valley? Did you go there before? You don't need to do another thing — it's already done so much for you. But they were right, because you can't build buildings, roads, bridges and houses if the people who live there don't benefit from it at all. Especially when you're talking about five of the most deprived areas in the UK, not just London, the UK. If you're going to spend £9 billion on it, then morally and practically, for the Treasury, and for good sense, you've got to make sure that education standards do go up, life expectancy does increase, wages go up and employment rates go up.

Michael Owens:

The rationale for the investment in the Games was that it would deliver a lasting legacy. Legacy is a malleable concept of course and measuring its impact requires taking account of the complexity of its consequences, from the creation of a parkland, the development of a group of new neighbourhoods, business areas, major sporting facilities, cultural and educational institutions, the relationship of all of it to the wider districts in physical and social terms, through to its impact on London and the nation.

When I arrived in the Lower Lea Valley in 1998, newly appointed as the Chief Executive of Leaside Regeneration Company, I was no stranger to dereliction and post-industrial decay. My career had exposed me to abandoned industrial sheds in Merthyr Tydfil and empty cotton mills in Bolton. The task of repositioning the west bank of the Lower Lea Valley, however, took some getting used to. The refrigerator mountains are fabled. We were able to buy Poplar Library for £1, but that was because it was in an advanced state of collapse, the interior detaching from the façade, and the entirety of the building and the land around it severed from the surrounding residential neighbourhoods by that ugly dual carriageway, matters made worse by the cleavages of railway lines, sewers, and pylons.

But the hidden economy was as rich and interesting as the equally hidden riverine landscape. What could this place become? How to talk of its revitalisation in a way that could speak to the needs of London and the local communities of Poplar and Bow? My imagination was fired by the vision for a Water City. As Paul Brickell explains above, this metaphor had been coined some years earlier by Reg Ward, the first Chief Executive of the LDDC. Water City captured the unique urban qualities of East London's riverine and former dockland area.

This powerful metaphor was mobilised to great effect in Newham's Arc of Opportunity. Water City was the ecological strand of the Council's vision: 'to restore a sense of the underlying natural order of the Lea Valley by forging a new series of water features through the urban fabric'. Like all good metaphors, its magic lay in its ability to communicate something greater than its literal meaning: 'the valley and its waters that should stimulate the collective memory and forge a greater sense of identity of the adjoining communities'.

The proposal to bid for an Olympics grew like a rising tide around 2001. A number of us locally were willing to open the flood gates: this would fit with our ideas. In 2002, I left Leaside and took a post in the newly formed LDA. In my mind, it would simply provide more resources for the existing regeneration work in the Lea Valley and possibly backing for an Olympic bid. I underestimated the forthcoming rupture, not just for me, but for the entire institutional landscape. The Olympics would sweep all before it: both the physical landscape and the institutional setting, permanently reforming both.

Did the Olympics engulf? In a certain sense, it did for me. I was closely involved in the master-planning at the bid stage, but the bid victory brought in new players and some formidable talents. I would leave for a while. But the tide turned, and I soon found myself back in the Lower Lea, now working as a consultant on plans for Stratford. I rediscovered Bow Arts Trust, a charity I encountered during my Leaside days. They had grown and matured. I began to work with the Trust and now I am a member of its Board. We have just taken a 999-year lease on commercial space overlooking the River Lea.

This book has shown that there was never actually a singular story. The project relied on multiple layers of action. Collaboration was everywhere, though it was not always intentional. The flow of purpose became impossible to resist. Like the flow of the River Lea itself, there were multiple river courses. The current became so strong for a period, but it would recede, and the eddies of the Bow Back Rivers would be revealed again. Now that the flood of the Olympic Games has receded, has it left the valley a better place? My answer is an unequivocal yes.

The Olympic Games provided the resources, expertise and institutional coherence to secure many components of the pre-Olympic plans that could never otherwise have been realised. Who could have imagined that 100 years of polluted soil would be washed, cleaned and returned to the ground, as it was in a 'soil hospital' for the site? Who would have conceived not only of an impounded, navigable waterway flowing underneath Stratford High Street, but also a stretch of the river that passes Zaha Hadid's breathtaking Aquatic Centre, open and serving the population?

The Olympics, like all mega-development, has reshaped economic and social life. Exclusion takes new forms, as does opportunity, and this development has created new opportunities in ways that have certainly stretched my imagination. The people of Newham, Tower Hamlets, Hackney and Waltham Forest do flood into the Park and its amenities. Not all the shoppers at Westfield arrive from Essex and Cambridgeshire; the shopping centre has a distinctly local ambiance: stand on the footbridge connecting new and old Stratford and witness the passers-by. The university and the bodies that form the growing cultural presence set out and succeed in drawing people from East London's schools and neighbourhoods.

I remember joining a curated walk through the Park with an artist shortly after the Games was over: a young entrant in the now thriving flaneur business. He wryly noted that the entire edifice, Stratford City and the Park's neighbourhoods, were built on the flood plain and London clay. Time would render this human aberration a temporary moment before the return of the marshes. His story was clever, well-crafted and funny but I cling to the hope that more young people will draw inspiration from the Victoria and Albert Museum, Sadlers Wells and the Universities rather than his nihilism.

The Olympic Park billions have not abolished inequality and some scepticism in empty rhetoric is healthy. But eye-watering investment has brought world leading institutions to this area. Now we can direct our energy to breaking down barriers and opening the doors, taking comfort from the fact that in this case many on the inside are keen to draw in those that remain on the outside. If I have to choose between the promise of London's growth and innovation in its productive economy, and a return to the clay and the marshes, I know which decision to make.

Jason Prior:

These big projects are incredibly intense. I went from 2003 to 2007, that's an amazing run on a job. Most people involved in conceiving an Olympic Games are gone within something like three months! We were all hugely passionate about it. There were clashing philosophical and intellectual approaches, but everyone was doing their best. You couldn't say that anyone was spoiling for the sake of spoiling. Everyone believed passionately. You have to admire all the plans, all the players. It was a big project that would never have happened at the level it happened without passionate belief, and passionate belief always generates passionate arguments.

In 2005 and 2006, when it was all over the shop and stuff was getting done, we couldn't afford to lose momentum. There was a bunch of us who were on this idealistic journey to push it as far as we could before reality kicked in, the whole thing stopped stretching and the elastic came whipping back at us. I think if we hadn't pushed it out that far, if we'd burrowed into a Treasury-prescribed position, we would be looking at something a lot meaner now.

The legacy transition of the Lea Valley is the best one I've ever seen. Munich was pretty good, but it was slow, it took a long time, whereas Lea Valley is bang-bang-bang. We're only three years out, and it's bloody impressive. It's a canvas on which things happen. And it will get better over time. Give it 20 years. Come back in 20 years.

Ralph Ward:

In 1994 I moved from the LDDC to GoL, joining John Sienkiewicz's small team working on London's planning and regeneration strategy. London's nether regions were top of our agenda, notably Stratford and the Lea Valley. The first meeting John asked me to attend was in the City, where the then Chief Executive of Newham wanted our support to help drum up commercial interest in their proposal for a station at Stratford on the Channel Tunnel Rail Link. 'Stratford International?', I said, slightly embarrassed. 'They can't be serious.' But they were. Very.

Around the same time, a regular visitor to our office in Millbank was Richard Sumray, with his idea of hosting an Olympics in the Lea Valley. He always left frustrated by our lack of enthusiasm. 'A distraction,' John used to say. 'If someone gave me billions to tackle East London deprivation, the Olympics is probably the last thing I would do.'

Prospective Olympic host cities always get very excited about 'legacy', but there is very little if any science that can make a connection between this short sporting event, however glossy, and durable urban and social change. There is not even any research evidence to suggest an increased take up of sporting activity in host nations even though it is always included as a legacy goal (London was no different). It is hard to escape the conclusion that legacy is more a matter of faith than fact. Most Olympic legacies are forgotten, amid sad images of empty decaying infrastructure.

Nevertheless, London took legacy particularly seriously, and literally. 'Let's make sure that the Olympic legacy lifts East London from being one of the poorest parts of the country to one that shares in the capital's growth and prosperity,' said Prime Minister David Cameron in his first speech to Parliament after being elected in 2010. His Government even made 'Olympic Promises' to that effect. At which point he allowed his Chancellor, George Osborne, to impose some of the biggest 'austerity' cuts in the country on the Olympic Host Boroughs, decimating the very local services that might have made a real difference to the welfare of local people. I call it the Marie Antoinette approach to urban renewal.

So, I have always been a bit of a sceptic about legacy. But I realise now that London has shown, through a combination of surprisingly good judgement, and extraordinarily good luck, that an event like the Olympics can create new directions for urban development and growth that are beyond most if not all conventional policy measures.

The good judgement was to locate the Olympics somewhere in London that had real though hidden commercial potential, a place where there was lots already being invested — and planned — in development and infrastructure, and a place where there was a real appetite for change. We might have taken the easy route and shunted the Games bid out to some godforsaken piece of vacant land in the 'Thames Gateway' in the belief that Olympic pixie dust (I have heard a Secretary of State use the term without irony) was sufficient to shoulder the whole burden of creating a new piece of city. In practice we chose perhaps the most difficult site we could find, full of occupants, saddled with power lines, massively contaminated, but full of opportunity, next to projected Crossrail and international rail connections and alongside advanced plans for the biggest urban shopping centre in Europe at Stratford City. Thanks, Richard Sumray and Mark Bostock. And Tony Winterbottom, Paul Brickell, Sandra Hunt, and the brave people behind Stratford City who we haven't yet mentioned: Stephen Jordan, property director at London and Continental Railways, and Nigel Hugill, Director of original developers Chelsfield. Take a bow. And not forgetting the sadly late John Sienkiewicz, who perhaps reluctantly, lies behind it all.

For London to choose Stratford as the location for such an international prestige event was astonishing. It turned on its head the establishment indifference and prejudice against East London that goes back hundreds of years, if not further. 'Londoners over the Border' as Charles Dickens called them in his excoriating account of the desperate social and environmental conditions in Canning Town in the mid-nineteenth century. When Joseph Bazalgette designed his giant Northern Outfall sewer to capture London's waste and redirect it away from the Thames in central London (and dump it, of course, further east), money was not made available to deal with the Lea as well, despite its hideous condition. Cholera outbreaks in East London traceable to the Lea were a regular feature of the Victorian era — the pandemic of 1866 killed 4000 in four months. You can still see the Northern Outfall Sewer vaulting indifferently over the Lea at Old Ford, just next to what is now the Queen Elizabeth Park. Perhaps the Olympics is East London finally getting the last laugh.

The good luck was twofold. Firstly, the success of the Games. This was not all good luck — quite a lot of sweat went into it, some of which we have managed to capture. But the flowers bloomed, the sun shone, the traffic flowed, medals were won, and the anti-aircraft missiles scattered about roofs of tower blocks surrounding the Park never had to be called upon. People still look back on the event with pleasure. Stratford, in London's, and local minds, is now no longer yesterday's place, a place of failure and decline, a place to escape. It is a place of success and pride.

The second piece of good luck, paradoxically, was that London never had a very clear plan of what to do with the site after the Games had finished, despite all the legacy rhetoric that surrounded the project. This gave it the chance to think through its legacy options again, more imaginatively, once the Games were over.

As ever with the Lea Valley, the original general intention was to build housing, as a gesture towards fulfilling the legacy promise to benefit local communities in a straightforward and uncomplicated way. But how much of the housing was really going to be affordable? And there are hundreds of less expensive sites available to build good housing in East London. This site is unique: there is nowhere else good enough to attract investment that can radically shift the direction of economic, business and cultural development of the area in entirely new ways. And that is what is happening. University campuses. Cultural icons. Here East Digital Business Centre.

The Olympics, unexpectedly perhaps, has created a place of the future, a place where businesses that might attract and support the area's young, fearless and creative population, can grow and prosper. It will take time; quite a lot of it. And more investment particularly in education, housing and local services. But we now have the launchpad, and I think we have ignition. So Mr Sumray — I guess you were right after all.

Index

A

Abercrombie's London Plan — 17
Aquatic Centre — 7, 97, 134, 151, 160
Arc of Opportunity — 12, 37, 38, 43, 44, 46-50, 52, 53, 69, 71, 76, 158
Arup — 11, 28-31, 33, 34, 66, 67, 69-71, 73, 79-81, 87, 104
Athlete's Village — 7

B

BidCo — 14, 83, 85, 86, 94, 95, 99, 103, 111, 112
Birmingham — 32, 37, 69, 78
Blacker, Gareth — 11, 68, 76, 102, 105, 106, 107, 109, 114
Bostock, Mark — 11, 28-30, 66, 70, 79, 163
Brickell, Paul — 11, 50, 53-55, 58, 63, 70, 74, 116, 123, 152, 158, 163
British Olympic Association — 16, 58, 66, 86, 113
British Rail (BR) — 14, 16, 30-32, 34
British Waterways — 13, 131-4
Bromley-by-Bow — 11, 21, 50-3, 63, 64, 70, 117, 119, 139, 141, 142, 153
Brown, Richard — 11, 53, 78, 93, 103, 111-13, 124, 125, 147
Burrows, John — 36

C

Canary Wharf — 22, 23, 28, 29, 36, 41, 51, 53, 61, 70, 93, 112, 117, 149, 150
Channel Tunnel — 11, 14, 15, 29, 31, 35, 36, 42, 67
Channel Tunnel Rail Link (CTRL) — 11, 14, 15, 26, 29, 30, 34-7, 40, 42, 43, 66, 91, 162
City Challenge — 26-8, 37-41, 45
Coleman, Neale — 12, 65, 72, 87, 95, 103-5, 118, 120, 123, 126, 128, 156
Compulsory Purchase Order (CPO) — 14, 23, 80, 99, 105, 106, 109, 110
Copper Box Arena — 7
Crossrail — 32, 163

D

Department for Communities and Local Government (DCLG) — 14, 17, 115, 120, 121
Department for Culture, Media and Sport (DCMS) — 11, 14, 16, 17, 61, 66, 79, 80, 81, 94, 95, 104, 115, 120, 121
Department of Trade and Industry — 16
Docklands — 16, 20, 22, 23, 26, 28, 31, 32, 40, 53, 70, 152, 154

E

Ebbsfleet — 31, 32
EDAW — 13, 15, 69, 75, 86-92, 98, 112, 134, 138, 140
English Partnerships (EP) — 15, 76, 78, 82, 121
European Regional Development Fund — 39
Eurostar — 14, 33, 34, 68

F

Fawcett, Eleanor — 12, 74, 131, 139

G

Government Office for London (GoL) — 15, 24, 25, 27, 83, 84, 98, 161
Graven, James — 12, 80, 81, 83, 85, 87, 88, 91, 92, 96, 97, 103, 104, 111, 113, 119, 121
Greater London Authority (GLA) — 11, 12, 15, 64, 71, 74, 75, 78, 82, 91, 93, 95, 98, 120, 126, 131, 139, 140, 141
Greater London Council (GLC) — 15, 20, 24
Greenwich — 37, 40, 41, 60, 88

H

Hackney — 12, 25, 61, 72, 77, 98, 127, 132, 135, 139-44, 151, 152, 160
Halcrow — 33
Hall, Peter — 28, 33
Heseltine, Michael — 26, 28-30, 33, 150
Hunt, Sandra — 12, 46, 48, 52, 64, 69, 73, 150, 163

I

International Olympic Committee (IOC) — 15, 67, 68, 92, 96, 97, 99, 101-3, 108, 111, 112

J

Jacobs, Steve — 26, 37, 45, 63, 76

K

Keith, Michael — 12, 19-21, 23, 26, 27, 30, 46, 48, 50, 53-5, 63, 74, 83, 149
King's Cross — 31, 32, 35, 96, 150

L

Lea Valley Partnership — 24-7
Lea Valley Regional Park Authority (LVRPA) — 13, 17, 95, 114, 115, 132
Leaside Regeneration Company — 11, 26, 50, 53, 55, 158
Livingstone, Ken — 11-13, 65, 72, 74, 77-9, 91, 96, 99, 109, 148
London and Continental Railways — 15, 33, 109, 163
London Development Agency (LDA) — 11-16, 55, 66, 68, 71-6, 78, 80-89, 91-9, 102-116, 119-122, 124, 125, 154, 159, 162
London Docklands Development Corporation (LDDC) — 13, 16, 22-6, 28, 36, 37, 42, 44, 50, 60, 62, 70, 154, 158, 161
London Legacy Development Corporation (LLDC) — 11-13, 16, 50, 70, 120, 122, 126, 143
London Organising Committee of the Olympic and Paralympic Games (LOCOG) — 16, 95, 111, 112, 116, 126, 147, 155, 168
London Thames Gateway Development Corporation (LTGDC) — 13, 16, 54, 141, 149, 152, 154
Lower Lea — 7, 11-13, 19, 20, 23-5, 27, 28, 30, 34, 37, 44, 48, 54, 55, 58, 64, 66, 69, 71-6, 81, 84, 88, 101, 104, 110, 123, 125, 131, 132, 134, 139, 140, 144, 149, 150, 157, 158

M

Mayor of London — 7, 11, 13, 15-17, 42, 59, 66-8, 71, 72, 74, 78, 79, 80, 81, 82, 83, 85, 91, 93, 94, 96, 98, 99, 115, 118-123, 125-8, 136, 141, 147, 148, 154

N

National Express — 33
Newham — 11-13, 16, 22, 25, 26, 29, 35, 38, 40, 41, 42, 44, 46, 48-50, 52, 53, 55, 62-4, 4, 69, 71, 73, 98, 109, 117, 118, 122, 128, 147, 158, 160

O

Olympic Delivery Authority (ODA) — 17, 69, 88, 94, 105, 106, 109-114, 116, 118, 120, 148, 152, 154
Olympic Park Legacy Company (OPLC) — 17, 71, 115, 120-126
Olympic Park Regeneration Steering Group (OPSRG) — 17, 115
Olympic Stadium — 7, 74
Opportunity Area Planning Framework (OAPF) — 17, 73, 75, 139, 140-143

P

Prescott, John — 29, 36, 91, 133
Prior, Jason — 13, 87-91, 112, 131, 134, 135, 137, 161

R

River Lea — 19, 22, 23, 43, 50, 52, 53, 128, 159
Rutter, Richard — 13, 131, 132

S

S G Warburg — 33
Shearer, Alan — 27
Sienkiewicz, John — 24, 27, 28, 161, 163
Single Regeneration Budget (SRB) — 17, 26, 51, 54, 132
Southwark — 16
Stratford — 11-13, 16, 19, 23-44, 46, 48, 50, 53, 61-3, 66, 70, 76, 79, 91, 101, 108-110, 136, 141, 142, 150-154, 156, 157, 159, 160, 162-164

T

Thames Gateway — 13, 16, 24, 27-30, 61, 74, 78, 81, 131, 154, 163
Tower Hamlets — 12, 13, 16, 20-27, 43, 44, 50, 51, 72, 73, 88, 98, 160

U

University College London (UCL) — 17, 50, 70, 118, 127, 128, 152

V

Velodrome — 7, 17, 138
Vikings — 19
Virgin — 33
Vivienne Ramsey — 13, 38, 49, 109

W

White Building — 12, 124, 140, 141, 143, 144
Whittle, Kevin — 13, 20, 23, 25, 27, 28, 149

Y

Young, Eleanor — 13, 72, 102, 103